itage
ok of
Avebury

English # Heritage
Book of
Avebury

Caroline Malone

B. T. Batsford Ltd/English Heritage
London

For Simon

7/90

CLITHEROE

034337810

Typeset by Lasertext Ltd, Stretford,
Manchester M32 0AH
Printed and bound in Great Britain by
The Bath Press, Bath
for the Publishers
B.T. Batsford Ltd, 4 Fitzhardinge St,
London W1H 0AH

ISBN 0 7134 5959 X (cased)
ISBN 0 7134 5960 3 (limp)

Contents

Illustrations

For their permission to reproduce photographs the Author's thanks are particularly due to:

English Heritage Alexander Keiller Museum, Avebury for figs 30, 32b, 34, 36, 37, 39, 44, 46, 47, 54, 70–72, 74, 77, 78, 84, 90, 92, 97–106 and 109.

Cambridge University Committee for Aerial Photography for figs 1, 7, 8, 23, 24, 51, 60, 64, 68, 73, 79, 82 and 95.

Bodleian Library for fig. 9.

Royal Commission on Historical Monuments for fig. 31.

Mick Aston for colour plates 5, 9.

D.O.E/English Heritage for fig. 28.

Colour plates

—1—
Avebury: the survival of an ancient landscape

This book is about the great Neolithic monuments of Avebury. It describes the evolution of Avebury through its archaeological remains and its historical records. There are two main elements to this story; the first is the world of the people who constructed the major remains in and around Avebury, and who left their imprint indelibly on the landscape. The second is an account of the subsequent destruction and the reconstruction of the Neolithic world of Avebury, including the role of the Roman, Saxon and medieval occupants, and the awakening interest of antiquarians and archaeologists from the seventeenth century onwards. Both elements combined provide a fascinating story, the first throwing unexpected light on a remote period of history, and the second on the emergence of the study of our ancient heritage.

There are few places in Europe where sufficiently comprehensive remains of ancient landscapes survive to allow a modern appreciation of our prehistoric past. Avebury in north Wiltshire is one rare survival, together with parts of Salisbury Plain around Stonehenge, the area of the Dorset Ridgeway near Dorchester, some of the moors of the Peak District of Derbyshire, tracts of Orkney and the moorlands of Dartmoor and Bodmin Moor. These are not simply natural landscapes of hills and trees, but are man-made remnants of entire planned territories, with the settlements and ceremonial monuments that formed the boundaries of what our prehistoric ancestors may have considered to be their civilized world (1).

By its very distance from the present, the prehistoric period is particularly difficult to comprehend. The time of the Romans – 2,000 years ago – seems remote enough, yet the

1 *Aerial view of Avebury in 1948, with Silbury Hill on the horizon.*

written records of that period give us insight into the thoughts and deeds of people otherwise as much buried in the depths of time as those of earlier societies. There is a considerable hurdle to be crossed, therefore, when considering prehistory, since there can never be the immediate contact with the past which we achieve when reading Tacitus, Plato or even Homer. Yet so substantial are the prehistoric remains we are considering, and so complete the landscapes of parts of the prehistoric past, that it is possible in ways which perhaps many people would hardly suspect, to appreciate something of the way of life and the organization of society thousands of years ago. Archaeology has

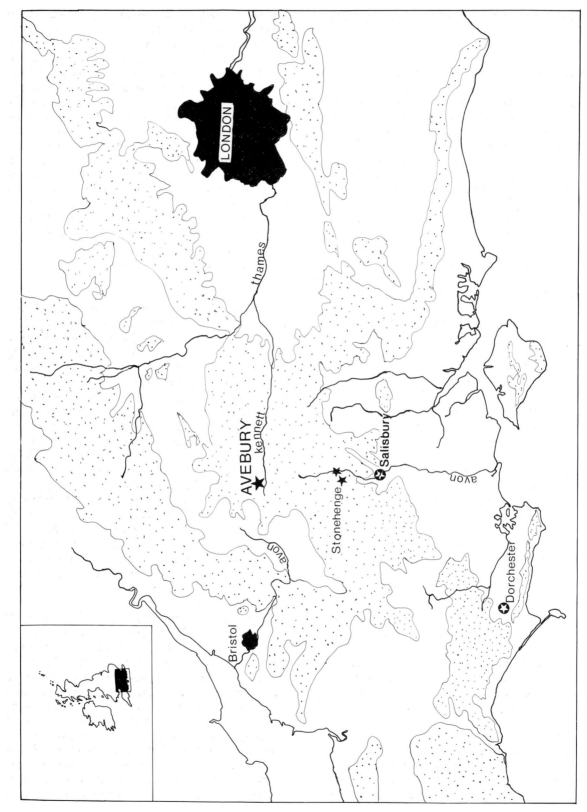

2 *General location map of the Avebury region.*

revealed so much hitherto unsuspected information about the monuments, about ancient technology, economy and burial practices, that some aspects of prehistoric life are readily accessible to us. Not everything by any means, can be reconstructed or known; we know nothing of the language or the family groups to which these ancient people belonged, but little more is really known about illiterate Roman or even medieval people. Evidence for unwritten history comes largely from the archaeological record. Once such evidence is imprinted in the ground, for instance in the form of building foundations, buried bones and the refuse of long-dead societies, it can be treated, recorded and analyzed. The interpretation of these kinds of evidence, although often tailored to suit different periods and places, is still essentially the same. Our knowledge of what was happening in the past comes from the study of material remains that have survived in the ground, as much as from surviving written records. The archaeologist's role is to recognise and try to reconstruct these material remains and to throw light on the society that deposited them hundreds or thousands of years ago.

The setting
In this book, the name 'Avebury' refers to more than just the modern village of that name, or to the great circle. It is used also to describe the surrounding area (**4**), and includes the modern parish which has a boundary on the east at the Ridgeway path, and incorporates East Kennet village to the south, and the hamlet of Beckhampton to the west. The northern limit is defined by Windmill Hill and the parish boundary of Winterbourne Monkton. In many respects this boundary is entirely arbitrary, and reflects merely the limits of what we can still identify as parts of the ancient landscape of Avebury, in spite of the superimposition of modern fields, villages, roads and trees which conceal and in some cases have partly destroyed the recognizable remains of the prehistoric landscape.

Avebury is located in North Wiltshire (**2**), on the western edge of the Marlborough Downs, and is some 20 miles (32 km) north of the great prehistoric complex that surrounds Stonehenge. But whereas Stonehenge is somewhat isolated within the chalk plateau of Salisbury Plain, Avebury stands at the headwaters of one of the most fertile river valleys, the Kennet, which flows east and north into the Thames Valley. Avebury also stands beside the ancient Ridgeway path, itself at least as old as the Neolithic landscape, and was thus located on what may have been one of the main communication routes of southern England 5000 years ago. It was near other similar centres such as Marden in the Vale of Pewsey, and the Stonehenge-Durrington-Woodhenge complex on Salisbury Plain; and not so distant from sites in the Cotswolds, Somerset and the Thames Valley such as Dorchester-on-Thames, and the comparable, if less well-understood areas in the Chilterns and central England.

Neolithic Avebury
The Avebury complex belongs almost entirely to the Neolithic period, between about 3710 BC (3000 bc) and 2000 BC (1600 bc) (see Glossary for explanation of bc and BC dates). During the 1500 or so years of construction and use at Avebury the surrounding landscape became one of the most important foci for ceremonial activities in southern England. First long barrows were built as tombs and shrines to the dead ancestors; then a causewayed enclosure was constructed on a hilltop already used for settlement and possibly for ceremonial activities. The three ditches and their banks enclosed a huge area of over 20 acres (8 ha), within which many communal festivals and events took place. There was feasting and the exchange of animals and gifts. Bodies were buried in shallow graves in the ditches, and the bones were later picked over and some, such as skulls and the long limb bones were used in rituals, apparently to honour the dead.

Soon after the completion of the Windmill Hill enclosures, the first of three wooden structures at the so-called 'Sanctuary' on Overton Hill was erected, and it too became a focus for the rituals which surrounded death and burial. The Sanctuary was then rebuilt, enlarged and finally built again in stone and linked with its standing stone 'Avenue' to the circle at Avebury. Before that occurred, however, Silbury Hill was built. The three different phases of its construction probably took several centuries to complete, and soon after Silbury attained its full height, the building of the great

Chronological table for Avebury

BC dates	Approximate uncalibrated bc dates	Period	Avebury Site	Other Sites, Culture, Economy and Landscape
4500	3520	Final Mesolithic		Nomadic hunting, gathering, fishing economy, wooded environment.
4300	3450	First Neolithic		The first clearance of forest, and agriculture established.
3800			Cultivation under Horslip Barrow.	Neolithic farming established in the Avebury area with ard ploughs.
3700	2950	Early Neolithic	Open settlement on Windmill Hill.	Avebury becomes a focus of settlement with Hamlets in the valleys and river terraces. Plain pottery and Neolithic tools in use.
			West Kennet long barrow constructed and the first burials in barrows.	Territorial barrows constructed marking the landscape boundaries.
3600			Cultivation under S. Street long barrow.	The landscape becoming cleared of woodland, with more fields and settlement.
3500	2725		Knap Hill enclosure built.	Large cooperative monuments such as the causewayed enclosures built. 3,000 BC
3400			S. Street long barrow built.	
3300		Middle Neolithic	Windmill Hill enclosures built.	
3200			Beckhampton barrow built.	Robin Hood's Ball causewayed site constructed.
3100				Stonehenge Phase 1 begun.
3000	2340		Square enclosure on Windmill Hill built, the Sanctuary begun.	Decorated Peterborough pottery in use, and new flint tool types introduced.
2900				

Chronological table for Avebury (*cont'd.*)

BC dates	Approximate uncalibrated bc dates	Period	Avebury Site	Other Sites, Culture, Economy and Landscape
2800		Later Neolithic		The landscape becomes degenerated, with growth of scrub, bracken and new woods.
2700			Sanctuary Phase 2.	Stonehenge Cursus constructed.
			Silbury Hill 1 built.	Grooved Ware pottery in use.
2600			? Avebury begun.	Windmill Hill declines in use.
2500	1950		Silbury Hill 2. Sanctuary Phase 3.	The henges of Marden, Woodhenge and Durrington Walls built.
			Silbury Hill 3	
2400		Final Neolithic.	? Avebury stones erected.	Beaker pottery introduced.
			Sanctuary Phase 3.	
			Avenues erected.	
2300			Sanctuary, Avenues and Avebury completed.	Long barrows cease to be used.
2200			West Kennet Barrow sealed.	The period characterized by ceremonial landscape and the regeneration of agricultural land with economic expansion to hills.
2100		Early Bronze Age.	Beaker burials on the Avenue and in Avebury.	Stonehenge bluestone circle constructed (Phase 2).
2000	1650			Stonehenge 3a sarsen circle constructed.
1900			Avebury sites begin to decline.	Later Beaker pottery and collared urns in use. The emergence of the Wessex culture.
1800	1500		Round barrows in use.	Stonehenge 3b built.

3 *Chronological table of the Avebury Neolithic period.*

stone circle at Avebury began, perhaps after 2400 BC (1950 bc).

This vast structure belongs to the class of monuments known as henges. These consist of a deep ditch and bank enclosing an almost circular area, often of substantial size, within which were circular buildings of wood and sometimes stone circles. Causewayed entrances through the bank and ditch allowed access to the interior of the henge, and in some places avenues of wooden posts, earthen banks or standing stones linked these entrances to other ceremonial sites nearby. At Avebury, the West Kennet stone avenue led from the stone circle to the Sanctuary over a mile away on Overton Hill.

The great henge and its stone circles formed the apex of the creation of the ceremonial landscape at Avebury. It was the focus of many communal events, festivals and ceremonies, some of which may have been concerned with seasonal events such as spring, harvest and winter, or with rites of passage associated with births, initiation rites, marriages and deaths. Although henges were not principally associated with the burial of the dead, scattered bones in the ditches, and the link via the stone avenue to what appears to have been a charnel house for human bones at the Sanctuary, suggests that death may have been one of the preoccupations of the rituals that were conducted within the circles of the great henge.

One of the features of the Neolithic monuments at Avebury is their great size. Compared with most other henges, causewayed enclosures, long barrows, artificial hills or standing stones, the Avebury monuments are huge. Elsewhere, although sites cannot compete with Avebury in size, they sometimes exploit impressive geographical positions. For example, the Knap Hill causewayed enclosure, some 5 miles (8 km) south of Avebury, although small, commands a spectacular position above the Vale of Pewsey. Nearby the Adam's Grave long barrow, although much smaller than either the East or West Kennet long barrows, makes up for its shorter length by its emphasis on height, achieved through its deep ditches at either side. The small size of the henge bank and ditch at Stonehenge was compensated for (at a much later date than the original construction of the henge) by the use of huge stones dragged into position from the Marlborough Downs, some 25 miles (40 km) distant.

Both from the remains that are visible today in the landscape of Avebury, and from a comparison of size or complexity with other ancient sites in Britain, it is clear that Avebury was always of prime importance. Its size, complexity, design and longevity of use, all attest that the Neolithic societies that created and used it, considered it to be one of their main centres. But a centre for what? There have been many theories about the sites and their meanings, perhaps none of them entirely satisfactory, for it is difficult for modern minds to comprehend exactly what motivated these people of the distant past. For some of us perhaps, one of the attractions of ancient sites is that we cannot know what precisely went on there or what the sites represented. But the monumental sites, their settings, and the archaeological materials excavated from them, provide a tangible glimpse of a remote and ancient world which we can struggle to understand, using all the clues which modern research makes available.

An Avebury chronology

A broad chronological framework for the area (3) allows us to place the individual sites in context, and shows that the story of Avebury is a continuing one from the arrival of farming communities in the area through prehistory to recent times.

The Neolithic period saw the first appearance of massive communal constructions. From the generations following the first land clearances around 4375–3500 BC (3500–2730 bc), the long barrows were built in a period that we know as the Early to Middle Neolithic. They represent the first major attempts to build enduring and monumental structures, intended both to impress the living, and to house the remains of the dead ancestors of the lineage systems of kinship that characterized early agricultural societies. Causewayed enclosures such as Windmill Hill were designed and constructed from about 3785–3000 BC (3000–2350 bc) and they must have been the first constructions in Britain that involved massive investments of labour from whole communities over many years. The Middle Neolithic period was characterized by these causewayed enclosures, and in its later phases by the first constructions of wood circles. Silbury Hill was built in the first centuries of the third millennium BC. On Salisbury Plain, the Stonehenge cursus (see Glossary) belongs to this period.

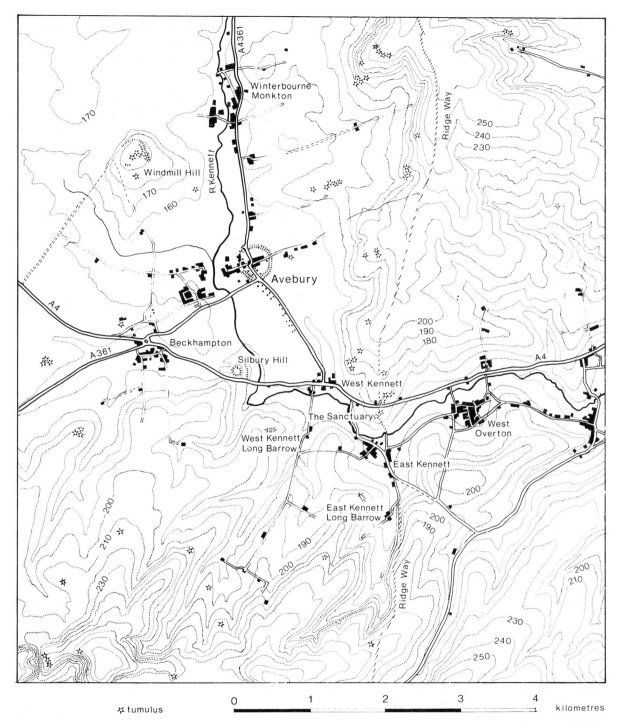

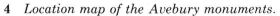
tumulus   0   1   2   3   4   kilometres

4 *Location map of the Avebury monuments.*

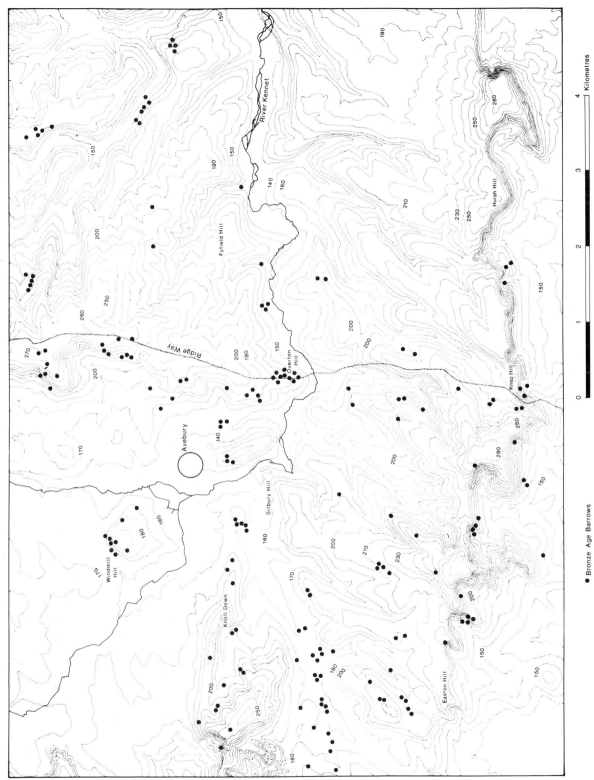

5 *Map of the Bronze Age landscape of Avebury, showing the round barrows.*

Artefacts reflect cultural and technological developments and thus provide a record of changes in society. Different forms of flint tools – of arrowheads, for example – reflect new flint knapping techniques and styles. In the early Neolithic period, pottery was typically plain, or very simply decorated, producing varieties such as the Hembury and Windmill Hill and early Fengate wares (36). The later Neolithic period is marked by changes in pottery decoration, with incised types such as grooved wares, Peterborough wares and other decorated styles appearing.

The later Neolithic period was also marked by a great increase in the numbers of massive communal and ritual monuments. These changes seem to represent a transformation of the social and economic systems. Typical monuments were the henges, stone and wood circles, long barrows, avenues of stone and earth, and the changes made to the megalithic entrances at the West Kennet and East Kennet long barrows when they were closed at the end of the Neolithic period.

Towards the end of the Neolithic period, copper tools were being introduced, and a type of pottery known as Beaker ware was in use. Individual warriors had special burials with grave goods. In comparison to the apparently egalitarian society of the earlier Neolithic periods, enormous social transformations had taken place. By about 2000 BC (c.1650 bc) a social hierarchy had developed and wealth and power, expressed through the possession of rare metal weapons, jewellery, and the construction of large ceremonial monuments, appear to have become dominating factors in society. Following the final Neolithic period, during the Early Bronze Age period from around 2000–1500 BC the same characteristics developed further and 'warrior-type' burials were increasingly placed under individual round barrows.

The evidence of the Middle Bronze Age (5), locally known as the Wessex Culture, is to be seen everywhere in the Avebury landscape, in the form of round barrows. These were built on the hilltops and crests of the chalk ridges, and were very numerous around Avebury and Stonehenge, as on Windmill Hill. In some cases, the burials were very rich, and the grave goods were of rare materials such as gold, glass and amber, modelled into items of great beauty, such as bronze daggers and tools, amber and glass beads, gold discs and lozenges, and jewellery.

Excellent examples can be seen in Devizes Museum.

By the Late Bronze Age (around 1100–900 BC), sumptuous graves and individual burial rites had begun to be replaced by the 'Urnfield' practice found on the Continent, of burial in large cemeteries in specially-made ceramic vessels. This is sometimes known as the Devrill Rimbury Culture, after a large cemetery in Wessex. Grave goods had become less important, although pottery, and special bronze items, such as jewellery and tools, were still placed in graves. In the Avebury area, some of the Middle Bronze Age barrows were used for inserting later urns. One example came to light in a barrow on Windmill Hill, when a rabbit warren disturbed the urn. It can now be seen in Avebury Museum (44).

The Iron Age period (6) can be seen all around the Avebury area in the form of Celtic fields and the earthworks surrounding the hillforts, such as at Oldbury Castle near Cherhill, and Barbury Castle south-east of Swindon. In particular, the chalk scarp above the Vale of Pewsey has many Iron Age fortifications and linear earthworks that must have formed a protective boundary to various territories. On Fyfield Down, Iron Age and Romano-British field systems can be clearly seen (7), showing that the upland areas were densely used for both settlement and agriculture.

During the Roman period, several villas were built in the Avebury area, along the fertile Kennet valley. Crossing through the territory was a substantial Roman road that linked the town of Mildenhall near Marlborough with Bath. It can clearly be seen today crossing the Ridgeway near the Sanctuary, and as both a cropmark and an earthwork in a stretch from Silbury Hill to the west of Beckhampton (8).

The Saxon period is represented principally by the construction of the great Wansdyke earthwork which extends from south of Marlborough west towards Bath. It appears to have been built as a territorial divide, perhaps between different native and Saxon groups. The Saxons later used Silbury Hill in their defence system, as a lookout and perhaps even as a defence point. The great circle of Avebury offered sanctuary inside its high bank and ditch. This may have been fortified in some way, and the name 'Waledich' or 'dyke of the Britons' was given to the prehistoric site. A large Saxon village grew up on the south-west side of the

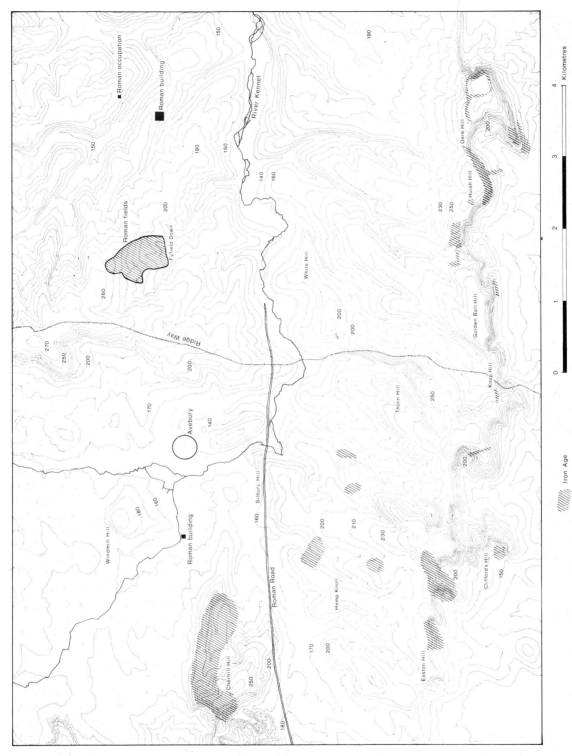

6 *Map of the Iron Age and Roman landscape of Avebury, showing surviving features.*

7   *Aerial photo of Fyfield Down prehistoric field systems, with scatters of sarsen stone littering the surface.*

8   *Aerial view of the Roman road passing to the south of Silbury Hill, showing as a faint line in the crops.*

circle, with substantial sunken floored timber buildings or 'Grübenhäuser'. Just to the north, a church was founded in the late Saxon period, probably in the ninth or early tenth century AD. The interior of the circle may have been the site of a fortified Saxon manor or palace, although there is little evidence for this.

Avebury was of little importance at the time of the Norman Conquest and received no mention in the Domesday records. It was first mentioned in assize rolls in 1289. However, before that time the church had been enlarged, and a Benedictine cell (succeeded by a small priory) was founded in 1114 to the north-west of the Saxon church. Soon after this the interior of the stone circle began to be used as a site for the village of Avebury, and at the same time the gradual destruction of the standing stones of the great stone circle began to take place.

John Aubrey, William Stukeley and the rediscovery of Avebury

Although most of the work of reconstruction of the monuments has been done in this century, and we owe most of our knowledge of them to recent excavation, much valuable information would have been lost for good without the interest taken in Avebury by two men, one in the seventeenth and one in the eighteenth century.

The initial rediscovery and the first surveys of Avebury were made by John Aubrey, a seventeenth-century antiquarian and a founder member of the Royal Society. He came across Avebury when he was hunting in 1649, and 'was wonderfully surprised at the sight of these vast stones of which I had never heard before'. He returned later to explore the area and sketch the monuments. After reading his written descriptions, Charles II asked to be shown the site in 1663, and instructed Aubrey to dig to see if he could find bones. Aubrey did not actually do any digging, but did make the first plain-*plane* table survey of the site, showing the position of many stones which were soon to disappear.

In 1663, the same year that Charles II, Dr Charlton and John Aubrey visited Avebury and climbed Silbury Hill, there was a meeting on the 8 July at the Royal Society. Both Aubrey and Charlton presented papers on the geometrical significance of the Avebury Circle, and these were accompanied by quite detailed sketch plans of the great site. However, both drawings showed the site to be a perfect circle, and all the arrangements of stones were set in exact geometrical alignment. Charlton even went so far as to show four stone Avenues, and Aubrey showed only the outer circle and a single, centrally placed inner circle. It would

9 *Stukeley's sketch of 'Atto de fe' or stone-burning at Avebury in 1724. The stonebreakers, the great pit, the straw and the stone fragments provide a vivid picture of the destruction by Tom Robinson, Farmer Griffiths and their colleagues (Bodelian Library, Oxford, Gough Maps 231).*

seem that these drawings were the result of philosophical argument, rather than observation on the ground. Aubrey's later plan showed the site as the irregular shape that we know today, and was the result of a systematic plane-table survey, not a speculative sketch from memory. Interestingly, the recent re-discovery of the 1663 plans has sparked off new discussion about what actually existed at Avebury. Thanks to the work of Gray and Keiller this century, we do not need to take the early sketches by Aubrey and Charlton too seriously, and should see them as part of the academic discussion of the seventeenth century that has developed into the archaeological science of this century.

Aubrey was a typical intellectual of his day, combining an interest in many disciplines, including history, art, archaeology, natural science and classical mythology. He regarded himself primarily as an 'antiquarian' or student of the 'antique', commenting 'Surely my stars compelled me to be an antiquary, I have the strangest luck at it, that things drop into my mouth'. He travelled widely in England, recording many ancient sites and buildings, preparing what was intended to be his *magnum opus, Monumenta Britannica*, a record of historic sites throughout the country. However, by the time he had completed the work he was impoverished and could not find a sponsor to pay for publication. The manuscript is now in the Bodleian Library. Aubrey's observations were fundamental, however, to the beginning of serious archaeology, which until then had relied heavily on classical mythology and pure fantasy. Aubrey recognised that there had been a period of 'prehistory' before the Romans, and that ancient sites like Stonehenge and Avebury belonged to that time. He considered Avebury to be of such significance that he wrote 'it does as much exceed in greatness the so reknowned Stonehenge, as a cathedral doeth a parish church'.

Besides his contribution to British archaeology, Aubrey is perhaps best known for his

10 *Stukeley's plan of Avebury showing where and when stones had been removed.*

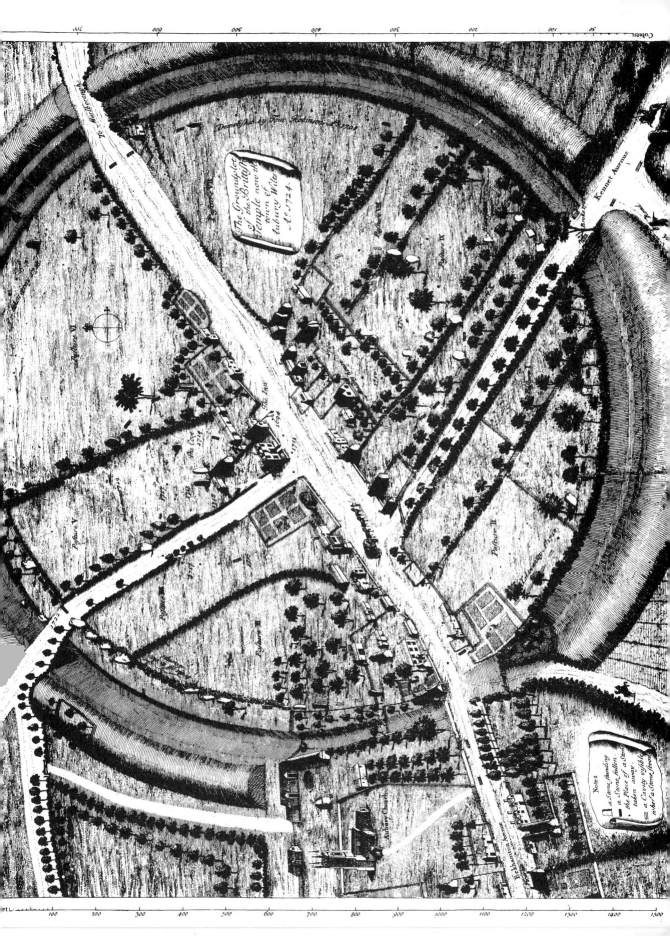

11 *Stukeley's sketch of the Cove in 1723.*

12 *Stukeley's sketch of the Obelisk in the southern circle.*

anthology of short biographies of his contemporaries, *Brief Lives*, which is a source of major importance for historians of the seventeenth century.

William Stukeley was originally a doctor of medicine, practising in London and Leicestershire, but became interested in ancient sites and architecture. He decided to travel about the country visiting antiquities and this led him first to Stonehenge and then in 1719 to Avebury. He visited the site again in 1720, and from then until 1724 spent much time there, recording all the monumental remains he could see. Although his interest had originally been aroused by Aubrey's account, Stukeley began to feel a strong proprietorial concern for the site, since no-one else had taken any interest in it, or sought to prevent its being damaged. Builders were now busy tearing down standing stones: Stukeley drew men like Tom Robinson the stonebreaker in action, and noted the dates when stones from the henge were destroyed (**10**) and their original positions. Fig. **9** shows Robinson at work in 1724.

Without Stukeley's work we should know very much less about Avebury, and indeed, it is arguable that had he not brought public attention to the site through his publication *Abury* in 1743, later antiquaries might have disregarded it altogether, allowing further destruction to take place. As Stukeley himself wrote, 'Since I frequented the place, I fear it has suffer'd; but at that time, there was scarce a single stone in the original ground plot wanting but I could not trace it to the person then living who demolish'd it, and to what use and where'. This was no small achievement.

However, not all his work was constructive, and his interpretation of the site became somewhat eccentric as the years went by. In 1729 he was ordained priest, and accepted the living of Stamford in Lincolnshire. By 1733 he had begun work on a study of the 'religion of the Druids and their temples and monuments'. Stukeley's interest in the Druids had first been aroused by the current intellectual habit of looking to the known classical past to suggest interpretations of less familiar areas of history – and thus to Roman authors' references to Druids. It is true that Aubrey had suggested in passing that Druids might have built Stonehenge, but he never took this idea as far as Stukeley did.

13 *Stukeley's sketch of the southern circle in 1723.*

A View of the South Temple July 15 1723.

In 1740 Stukeley published a book on Stonehenge, which although focussing on fictitious Druid associations, nevertheless identified and named many outlying sites on Salisbury Plain as well as recording the Stonehenge complex itself. In 1743 *Abury – a temple restored to the Druids* was published, and in it Stukeley set out his interpretation of Avebury, in which he saw the monuments forming the outline of a giant serpent. Since Stukeley's day the association in the popular mind between Stonehenge, Avebury and the Druids has never been lost. In 1781 the 'Ancient Order of Druids' was founded, and prehistoric stone circles were from then on to be bound up with Druid rites, sun-worship, astronomy and magic. Even today 'Druids' gather at Midsummer at Stonehenge to conduct 'ancient' ceremonies, which in fact have no earlier authority than the late eighteenth century.

The visible remains

It is not the intention of this book to provide an armchair guide to the Avebury sites, but instead to interpret for the reader some of the information that has survived at Avebury. There is no substitute for visiting Avebury and exploring its landscape. It provides one of the best examples of a monumental neolithic landscape, and once it has been appreciated, other less spectacular or well-preserved fragments of our ancient past can be discovered and enjoyed. However, this is a past now under threat. In the last generation or so, massive landscape change has occurred, partly through the increased mechanization and intensification of agriculture, with deep ploughing, land drainage and earth levelling, all destroying ancient landscapes. EEC subsidies and the economic climate of the past two decades have ensured that only monuments protected by law, by responsible landowners or under traditional farming regimes have survived unscathed. However, even more destructive to the remains of the past is the process of urban expansion, with the creation of massive roads and industrial sites, quarries and housing estates. Obviously the present needs of our society, and all the changes and developments that this entails, cannot be halted just to preserve traces of the past landscape for our interest.

Even the famous landscapes of Stonehenge and Avebury are under threat. Most of the fields around the sites are under intensive cultivation, and many barrows or settlements are now flattened and buried under the disturbed ploughsoil. The slopes of Windmill Hill, once perhaps the site of early Neolithic settlements, are anonymous cornfields. The line of the West Kennet Avenue, beyond the reconstructed northern portion, has been deep-ploughed annually, and any stones that might have been there are probably broken and shifted far from their original positions. There are frequently planning applications to build and extend houses in the near vicinity of the monuments. Each time land is ploughed or a new building erected, a little more evidence of the past is lost, even though archaeological observations are usually made. Even if these developments are designed to cause the least destruction possible, the landscape is changing inexorably, and the archaeological clues to the past grow fewer every year.

2

The environment of Neolithic Avebury

The landscape of Avebury is that of typical southern British chalkland, with undulating hills cut by small streams rising from the base of the chalk hills, forming fertile valleys. Avebury stands on the western edge of the Marlborough Downs, a high ridge of chalk that runs north-eastwards to the Berkshire Downs and to the Chiltern Hills. To the south, the chalk plateau of Salisbury Plain rises as an undulating tableland, divided from the Marlborough Downs by the fertile Vale of Pewsey. To the north of Avebury, the chalklands end abruptly at the scarp edge of the Thames valley. To the west, the chalk is replaced by the oolitic limestone of the Bath and Cotswolds region. The high chalk ridge of the Marlborough Downs is exploited by the ancient Ridgeway, a major route from the earliest Neolithic period. The Thames valley to the north also provides an easy route east to west. In many respects, Avebury, within 7–10 miles (11–16 km) of the headwaters of the rivers Kennett and the Bristol and Salisbury Avons, is at a crossing point or junction between several natural regions – on the watershed, between east and west, north and south.

On a geological time scale, the chalk landscape of Wiltshire is comparatively recent, and was formed only some 100–65 million years ago, under what were then marine conditions. The chalk itself was formed from the calcareous residues of minute marine animals and corals, and was laid down in thick distinctive layers, which everywhere are more than 660 ft (200 m) thick. The chalk itself is a very pure form of calcium carbonate, and is a soft, friable material, which nevertheless is surprisingly resistant to erosion through its porous nature, allowing water to pass through it rather than scraping away the surface. Thus the main chalk hills remain high and well-defined throughout most of southern England.

There are three main bands or layers making up the chalklands – upper, middle and lower chalk – each of different composition, and thus forming different landscape features. The lower chalk has a high clay content (10–50 per cent) with the higher percentages of clay in the base layers, making an impervious layer on which water collects, and forming springs along the base of the hills. Middle chalk contains between 5–10 per cent of clay-marl, and forms the main scarp slopes under the harder capping of upper chalk. The upper chalk is the purest variety, and forms the bulk of the visible chalklands as undulating downland. Flints are found mainly in this layer, and most of the prehistoric flint mines exploited seams which lie at the base of the upper chalk.

In the context of prehistoric Avebury, (14) the different layers of chalk making up the landscape were of considerable importance, because the different landforms could be exploited for different purposes. Avebury itself sits on a prominent lower chalk 'cuesta' or inclined plain. It forms a nearly flat plateau-like area, ideally suited for the ceremonial centre of the stone circles. Windmill Hill on the other hand is formed by an outlier of upper and middle chalk, and thus stands high above the surrounding ground, commanding good views over Avebury and the Kennett valley.

The Marlborough Downs, which dominate the horizon to the east of Avebury, are formed from a well-preserved block of upper chalk. The Ridgeway path along its western crest was in use from early times, and Neolithic communities quickly exploited its strategic position. Besides

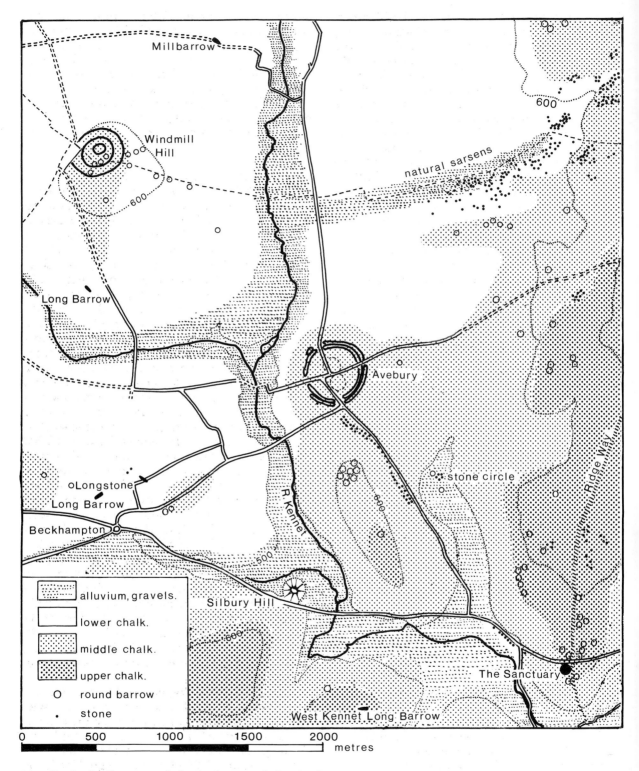

14 *Geological/geomorphological map of the Avebury area.*

being a major north-south route, the Marlborough Downs were a rich source of sarsen stone, from which both Avebury and Stonehenge, and many other prehistoric monuments were built. The sarsens once formed a hard silicaceous sandstone layer or duricrust over the chalk, probably laid down under hot desert conditions in the Upper Eocene and Oligocene geological periods, between 65–26 million years ago. The blocks were then broken up into boulders by earth movements and natural erosion, into the blocks that still cover Fyfield Down, Clatford Bottom and Piggledene. Most of the blocks are no more than 7 ft (2 m) in length, although massive stones up to 21 ft (6 m) long and weighing 59–69 tons (60–70 tonnes) were dragged down to Avebury and Stonehenge for the construction of the circles. The surface of the standing stones at Avebury and on the downland nearby is rough in texture, with holes and rivulets covering much of them. These may have been formed by the roots of desert plants, living in what was originally a sand desert, and by stream and wind erosion millions of years ago. Further erosion has taken place since, as some of the supine boulders show. The local name for the sarsens is 'greywethers' since the stones often look like flocks of grazing sheep on the hillsides.

Broken nodules of flint cover the surface of every field in the chalklands. These are derived from the layers of flint eroded out of the chalk, laid down over thousands of years when it was deposited as a marine sediment. The flint was formed as a minute crystalline structure in the upper layers of chalk, from the remains of marine organisms and sponges. These organisms were trapped in the layers of calcareous matter that formed under the sea, and absorbed silica through a process of precipitation, until they became hard shiny flint. The surface of flint appears white and rough, and is called the cortex. This was formed when the surface water content of flint was removed, leaving air spaces which then absorbed calcium from the surrounding chalk. Many prehistoric flint tools show a layer of the cortex. The best flint for making tools was mined from seams in the upper chalk, and in some parts of Britain, prehistoric mines such as that at Grimes Graves in Norfolk still survive from the Neolithic period.

Flint provided an ideal material for toolmaking because when broken into blades through a skilled method of knapping, it was brittle, sharp and workable. Flakes produced from cores could then be finished off by working the edges to form specific tools such as knives, sickles, chipped axes and arrowheads. Flint could also be polished and ground to make a smooth cutting edge on knives and axes. The range of Neolithic artefacts produced was very extensive and well-adapted to the great variety of different needs required by an agricultural economy.

The Neolithic period

The Neolithic period is probably the most significant in the history of man. The adoption of agriculture, and the related cultural changes that went with it, allowed social and economic developments at a rate that was unparalleled before. The Old and Middle Stone Age hunting, gathering and fishing communities, adapted to their environments, and exploited whatever resources they could, in a world of steadily changing glacial and interglacial climates. This period of man's history is known as the Palaeolithic and Mesolithic periods and lasted from c. 4 million years ago with the first appearance of hominids in Africa, to about 10,000–7000 years ago. The glacial hunters tracked game, such as reindeer, bison, musk-ox, mammoths and other mammals along the fringes of the frozen wastes. Once these ice sheets melted (around 10,000 years ago) the coastlines were exposed as vast areas of estuary and marsh, and the hunters adapted a different way of life to the new conditions, developing skills as fishermen, mollusc gatherers and hunters of small game such as sea mammals, birds, deer and small land mammals. This Mesolithic or Middle Stone Age period was one of increasing economic stability, and camps were often of long duration and close to predictable food supplies. The islands of Britain supported a remarkably rich Mesolithic population, and sites were located along coasts and rivers throughout the British Isles. Small, light flint blades were made into harpoons, knives and composite tools for processing vegetables and meat.

The waters once trapped in the great glacial ice masses continued to melt and the seas rose inexorably, drowning the river and coastal estuaries that had supported the thriving Mesolithic populations of Britain and north-west Europe around 8000–9000 years ago. Until this time, Britain had been intermittently connected to Europe during the glacial and interglacial periods by a low-lying landbridge. This was submerged by the rising sea levels, finally turning Britain into an island.

At much the same time, critical changes were taking place in the Near East. In the area known as the Fertile Crescent between Iran, Iraq and Turkey, wild grasses were evolving into viable cereals that produced substantial seed heads. The changing climates associated with the end of the Ice Age also affected comparatively warm areas of southern Europe and the Near East. The hunter-gatherer communities of these areas were forced to look for alternative sources of food, and the evolving species of cereals, peas and beans, together with wild cattle, sheep, goats and pigs, formed a new food supply. The handling, controlled breeding and artificial conditions under which these animals were kept allowed their gradual evolution into what we now recognize as domestic species of cow, goat, sheep and pig. Their sizes, teeth patterns and horn formations, and their productivity of milk, meat and wool all changed under the control of man. Cereal grains were sown and harvested, and because this required a substantial investment of time and effort, the emerging farming communities gradually settled by their fields rather than wandering nomadically. Village communities developed throughout the Near East and south-eastern Europe, and the former nomadic way of life was continued only by shepherds and traders.

Although early farming must have been laborious and often unpredictable, it led to the formation of permanent settlements and the production of steady food supplies. It allowed the populations that practised agriculture to expand, and there is very clear evidence throughout the Near East and south-east Europe of rapid population growth. With this came the need to expand the territory used for crops and for animal grazing, and slowly but steadily, Neolithic farmers gradually moved westwards from the Fertile Crescent towards Europe. In their progress, local bands of Mesolithic hunters and gatherers were either absorbed into the developing agricultural communities, or pushed into the marginal areas of uplands and coasts. This whole process took perhaps some 4000 years before it actually reached Britain. Once it did, and agriculture was introduced, the change was rapid and lasting. Even communities in the most marginal areas, such as the Scottish islands, soon adopted the practice of husbandry

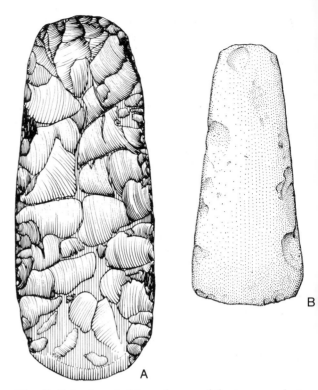

15 *Polished and chipped axes of the type used at Avebury to clear trees throughout the Neolithic period.*

with the domestication of plants and animals. After 4000 BC (3250 bc) Britain had its own thriving farming communities who began to clear the forests to make fields and pastures. It was in this newly-made landscape that the social developments took place which resulted in the building of the great Neolithic monuments.

Environmental changes

Much evidence survives in the soil that allows us to reconstruct the environment of the first farmers. Pollen grains from various trees and plants are often preserved in damp, peaty conditions. The most common trees in lowland Britain were oak, birch, hazel and alder, together with elm, beech and lime and other native species. The nature of these trees indicates that the environment of lowland Britain when first encountered by the early Neolithic farmers was dominated by damp, heavy soils and that there was thick forest cover in many areas.

Pollen studies of buried prehistoric soils have shown that the early farmers soon cleared great tracts of the landscape of the forest cover, probably using a slash and burn technique that rapidly opened up large clearings in the forested areas. In a relatively short period the proportions of pollen grains from trees, rather than from grasses and cereals, declined markedly. Oak and elm in particular were replaced in some areas of new clearance by grasses and cereals.

It is possible to date the clearance of the landscape through the use of radio-carbon dating. This method uses the faintly radioactive component known as Carbon 14 (C14) of organic remains such as charcoal, peat, wood or bone to provide a date by measuring its rate of decay. All living things contain the natural isotope C14 at a roughly consistent level. When they die, the C14 decreases at a steady and measurable rate. Consequently, organic, or once living materials can be measured for the quantity of C14 that they contain. Their 'radio-carbon age' can then be calibrated against a calendar produced from dates derived from wood samples dated by tree rings. An absolute and a calendar date can then be calculated. Usually such dates

have to be expressed in terms of probability, and in the form '4000 ± 100' showing that the sample has a 90 per cent change of falling within the limits of the period specified (see Glossary).

Buried soils, peats or archaeological deposits associated with preserved pollens are sometimes associated with C14 dates taken from small pieces of charcoal or peat and can thus date the landscape changes that man was initiating around 4000–4250 BC. Studies of ancient soils preserved under prehistoric earthworks provide good evidence to show that the natural environment of modern England is very different from that of the Neolithic period. Most changes appear to have been caused by human intervention, although climatic changes may also have caused leaching, soil erosion, and subtle vegetational change. Snail shells pre-

16 *Schematic reconstruction of the first Neolithic landscape of Avebury, showing the natural forest with small clearings and agricultural plots and the location of early settlements (after R.W. Smith 1984).*

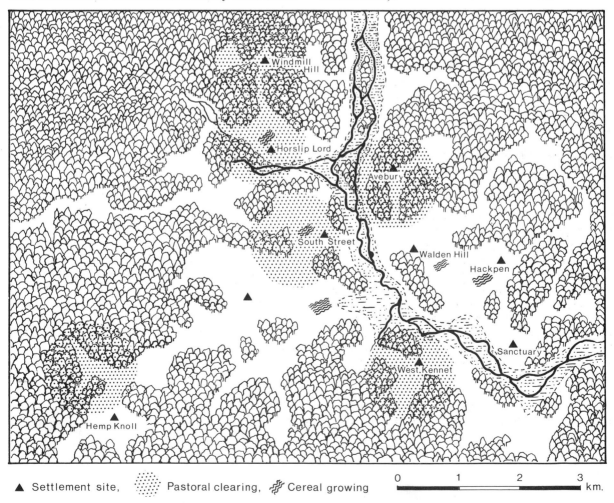

▲ Settlement site,   ⣿ Pastoral clearing,   ⚘ Cereal growing

served in ancient soils also provide evidence of different local conditions before and during the Neolithic period. Different snails have marked preferences for different types of habitat, and some species are only found in very restricted environments, such as undisturbed woodlands, ponds, and open heathland. What is more, snail shells are almost indestructible; small, but recognizable fragments removed from prehistoric contexts can indicate the sort of environmental conditions that prevailed around prehistoric sites with some precision. The chalky soils around Avebury rarely preserve much pollen, and snail shells therefore provide the best environmental data. Thanks to John Evans, who has been making a study of the Avebury region using these methods for over two decades, the area is now one of the best understood prehistoric landscapes in Britain.

The initial process of forest clearance in the early Neolithic period was probably one of 'slash and burn', where large areas of old woodland were cut down and then burnt by the first communities that decided to settle in the area. This primary phase of Neolithic intervention is sometimes known as the 'clearance phase'. The cutting and burning allowed the cleared areas to become rapidly transformed into grasslands. Grazing animals would have prevented much regrowth of the original forest. This phase was predominantly one of pastoral farming with only small, unrestricted areas of especially fertile and light soil being cultivated. These were probably located near to the settlements, on the terraces above the streams, and may have looked rather like allotments or vegetable gardens (16). There may have been extensive settlements on the lower slopes of Windmill Hill, but all around Avebury, the upper hillsides were still covered in thick 'climax' woodland, the dense oak woodland which existed in the earliest prehistoric period. However, the general lack of settlement evidence for Neolithic Britain may be explained by the likelihood that many settlements were on the alluvial lowlands and terraces. These locations have since become covered with layers of silty soil washed down from the surrounding areas, which would completely cover earlier settlement traces, often with several feet of soil.

The Neolithic period was one of technological change, partly brought about through the changing needs of a food-producing economy, and partly through the cultural changes developed by a newly sedentary society, settled firmly in one place throughout the year. The most significant tools that enable man to clear and cultivate the landscape were chipped and polished stone and flint axes and the development of simple ploughs or 'ards' (see Glossary). The axes were made from large pieces of stone or flint which were then chipped into shape, and the cutting edge, and sometimes the whole surface, polished to a sharp edge and smooth finish. Once hafted into a solid wood or antler handle, the axe provided an excellent tool, which for the first time made it possible to cut down quite large trees (15).

Similar chipped tools, called adzes, were given larger wooden handles and used like hoes for cultivating the soil. Ploughs and ards developed during the Neolithic period, and it is clear from evidence found under the South Street long barrow at Avebury that ploughing was taking place here before 3600 BC (2800 bc). Under the barrow, a dense pattern of scratch marks was found in the buried soil, formed by a plough or ard passing to and fro across the site (17). Since there was only a single criss-cross pattern of marks, it is likely that the ploughing was done only once, to break up the soil surface when the site was first cleared and cultivated. These marks are the earliest evidence in Britain for plough cultivation. A wooden ard, perhaps like

17 *Ard marks found beneath the South Street long barrow at Avebury.*

18 *Sketch of the Neolithic ard found at Donner-upland in Denmark (after Fowler).*

the one used at South Street, has been found preserved in a Danish bog at Donnerupland. Ards were probably of composite construction and the plough tip or share was either made from wood, hardened by fire, or perhaps made from chipped flint or stone (**18**). The South Street long barrow site also revealed important environmental information about the earlier Neolithic period in the Avebury area. The mound had been constructed over the existing soil, thus burying it and allowing all the mollusc remains to be preserved intact. The earliest fauna in the soil were associated with a wind-deposited layer that suggests an open tundra-like landscape with no trees. Above this were tree holes associated with temperate woodland snails which lived amongst the roots and trunks. This phase was associated with the spread of forest across the Wiltshire downland during the post-glacial period. Then came signs of man's first intervention in the area: the criss-cross grooves of the plough which scored the sub-surface of the soil soon after the trees were first cleared from the landscape. The ploughed land was then allowed to revert to grassland for a time: the snails, found in the buried turf layer provide firm evidence for this episode. The barrow was then constructed over this small fragment of landscape history, sealing it completely, at about 3580 BC (2800 bc).

Initially, the cleared landscape was fertile, and large productive areas were cleared over the earlier to middle Neolithic period farming large tracts of semi-open ground, fields and grazing (**19**). However, the humus-rich forest soils were easily eroded and leached of their essential minerals through over-cultivation, and became generally degraded, much as soils in the tropical forests of the Amazon are today. In the Avebury area during the Neolithic period

it is possible to identify three broad phases of landscape change related to the changing fertility of the soil. Initially only the prime soils, such as the terrace silts, were used for cultivation, but as the population grew, and agricultural methods became better adapted to the chalklands, more marginal areas were taken into agricultural use. This appears to have led to a gradual degeneration in the quality of the soil and its productivity, probably through over-use and lack of crop rotation. A period often known as the 'phase of abandonment' can then be identified, when quite large areas of the Avebury landscape reverted to a scrubby vege-tation of plantain, weeds, bracken, thorn bushes and other wasteland plants (**20**). This was fol-lowed by a third phase, of woodland regener-ation, with a predominance of birch trees and the return of oak woodland. By the end of the Neolithic period, the landscape was probably less fertile than it was when farming first began in the area. However, this was compensated for by more extensive farming methods, with a great increase in grazing animals such as cattle and sheep on the higher downland which had now become included in the agricultural terri-tory. Open landscape can be identified from environmental studies. At the same time, new types of crop and farming methods also helped to increase productivity in the original farming areas around the settlement. Nevertheless, this landscape degeneration may have led to eco-nomic stress, and may have been one of the causes of the social change which can be detected later in the Neolithic period. This social change appears to have manifested itself in the building of massive communal monu-ments, in warfare, in a new emphasis on status of individuals, and in a new type of social structure.

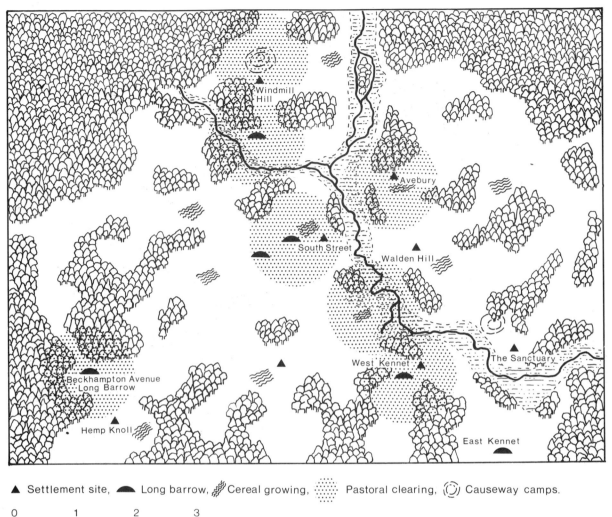

▲ Settlement site, ⬛ Long barrow, 🌾 Cereal growing, ⣿ Pastoral clearing, ⊚ Causeway camps.

0   1   2   3
km.

19 *Schematic reconstruction of the early–middle Neolithic landscape of Avebury, showing the increased clearance of the forest, with large plots for grazing and cereal crops, together with the long barrows (after R.W. Smith 1984).*

Elsewhere in Britain, the clearance and abandonment phases cannot be identified as clearly as at Avebury; instead more marginal upland areas suggest shifting cultivation with sucessive phases of forest clearance. Elsewhere, as on the Somerset Levels, the forests were exploited through coppicing, and through grazing animals on the trees.

Materials used in the monuments

The prehistoric monuments were constructed mainly of local materials, such as chalk rubble, earth, flints and sarsen stones. However, small quantities of more exotic materials, often from considerable distances, were collected and built into the monuments, perhaps for ritual or symbolic reasons. Such materials include Jurassic limestone from the Calne area to the west of Avebury, found in the square enclosure on Windmill Hill, on the Sanctuary, along the West Kennet Avenue, and built into the chambers of the West Kennet long barrow. The most spectacular use of exotic stones is, of course, the famous bluestones at Stonehenge, which were brought from the Prescelly mountains of south Wales via the River Avon to Salisbury Plain.

Neolithic communities were not parochial, in

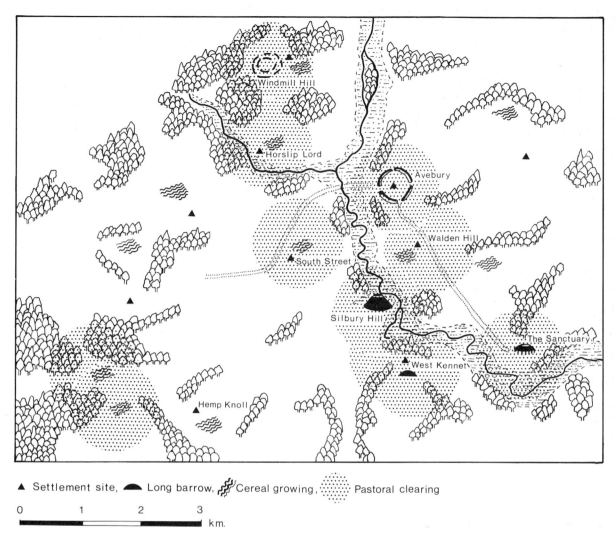

▲ Settlement site, 🔺 Long barrow, 〰️Cereal growing, ⋯ Pastoral clearing

0   1   2   3
                    km.

20 *Schematic recontruction of the later Neolithic landscape of Avebury showing the woodlands cleared, but reverting to hazel scrub and bracken. Extensive agricultural areas were used for crops and animals, especially pigs (after R.W. Smith 1984).*

spite of their sedentary domestic lifestyle. They were fully aware of the natural resources in their own areas, and in many other parts of Britain. This is well demonstrated by the extensive trade networks which have been identified through the chemical analysis of stone axes. These were mined in many parts of northern and western Britain, such as the Lake District, north Wales and Cornwall. The smaller stone axes may also have had more than a utilitarian value, and were perhaps especially prized for

their rarity, colour, cutting quality, and perhaps for their exotic nature. These exotic objects, including rare shells, stone objects and pottery as well as the imported axes, and perhaps also the monuments built from imported stone may have been the preserve of a small elite group within the Neolithic community, having a symbolic value because of their rarity and their association with high-ranking people. At Windmill Hill, a very wide variety of imported polished axes were found from all parts of western and northern Britain, far more than at other comparable sites. This may indicate the importance of the Avebury area in terms of the trade networks that operated in prehistoric Britain. As well as the ordinary exchange of goods such as pots, flints, and axes, there could have been an elaborate system of gift exchange between

21 *Reconstruction of an earlier Neolithic landscape at Avebury, with forest clearance, small fields and settlements (Judith Dobie).*

various groups of people who may have been related through kinship and other ties. The causewayed enclosures may have functioned as meeting places when such groups came together.

The landscape of Avebury still offers much scope for further investigation. Only limited field survey has been carried out around Avebury, and this has not been associated with more extensive landscape studies. Small contributions each add a little more knowledge, but a study of the whole Avebury area, similar to the work recently carried out at Stonehenge, is urgently needed. For example, we still have little idea about the pattern of settlement in the area at any given phase of the Neolithic period, and many aspects of more modern archae-

ological research has never been applied to the major monuments. No samples of soil have been studied from under either the West or East Kennet long barrows; or from under the bank or from the base of the ditch of Avebury itself; so we still know little about the environment at the time of their construction, or indeed about the phases of construction and use of the monuments themselves. There are still very few radio carbon dates from the Avebury area, and chronology of the whole Neolithic period probably needs revising. Each decade brings new archaeological and analytical techniques which add information to the history of Avebury, and the present picture can only be a short-term view.

3

Avebury and its monuments

The establishment of a secure and reliable Neolithic economy during the earlier centuries of the fourth millennium BC (4000–3500 bc) provided the basis upon which the building of the major monuments of Neolithic Britain was possible. Prehistoric sites of this nature, whatever their layout and plan, are constructions built for effect, be it social or economic, practical or decorative. They are sites that have a function beyond that needed for everyday survival. Thus for societies to expend valuable time, energy and resources on such building, there must be a fairly secure and predictable economic base. It is not unknown in various parts of the world for very simple hunting and gathering societies to erect stones, build tombs and other structures, but these are rarities. It is more usual to find monument builders amongst well-established agricultural societies, and in north-west Europe, this was the situation after about 3700 BC (3000 bc).

Within the prehistoric landscape of Avebury, the man-made remains are all monumental, making Avebury and its surroundings a ceremonial and ritual complex of some sophistication – a 'monumental landscape'. They are large, highly visible monuments and in the context of the Neolithic world to which they belong, highly labour-intensive. Many people must have been working on the sites for large proportions of the year, and doing little else.

The territory of Avebury has certain components which are commonly shared with other surviving Neolithic landscapes. These are: a causewayed enclosure (Windmill Hill); long barrows (West and East Kennet, South Street, Horslip, Beckhampton); a henge (Avebury); stone circles (the Sanctuary and the smaller peripheral circles); an avenue (the West Kennet Avenue) and other structures that were placed

in the landscape for visual effect (for example, Silbury Hill). At Stonehenge, all the same components exist, in a different arrangement and constructed with a different emphasis. Silbury Hill is not repeated; instead there is the Cursus. There is a causewayed enclosure (Robin Hood's Ball); and three henges (Stonehenge, Woodhenge and Durrington Walls). There are also numerous long barrows, Bronze Age round barrows, and an avenue of earthen banks. Smaller circles are present, but represented in wood, at Durrington and Woodhenge. In the Dorchester (Dorset) area, similar monuments are again found, with a causewayed enclosure at Maiden Castle, a henge on the edge of Dorchester (later converted into a Roman amphitheatre) with smaller circles within, and there are long barrows in profusion, but no obvious avenue.

In fact, wherever there is reasonable survival of some of the elements of a monumental Neolithic landscape, it is possible to identify other elements of what is becoming recognized as a familiar repertoire. Indeed, such is the advance of knowledge in recent years about these ancient landscapes, that it is possible to claim that most henges and causewayed enclosures were once related to other sites of a nature similar to those which survive at Stonehenge and Avebury, that made up what we now consider to be ceremonial, or indeed ritual centres in a landscape that was prepared and planned by the farmers who first occupied it.

The slow evolution of Neolithic landscapes, of which Avebury is one, happened in a certain order, reflecting the gradual social and economic changes which were taking place. The earliest constructions (dating from the early Neolithic period) were the long barrows and the causewayed enclosures, some of the barrows

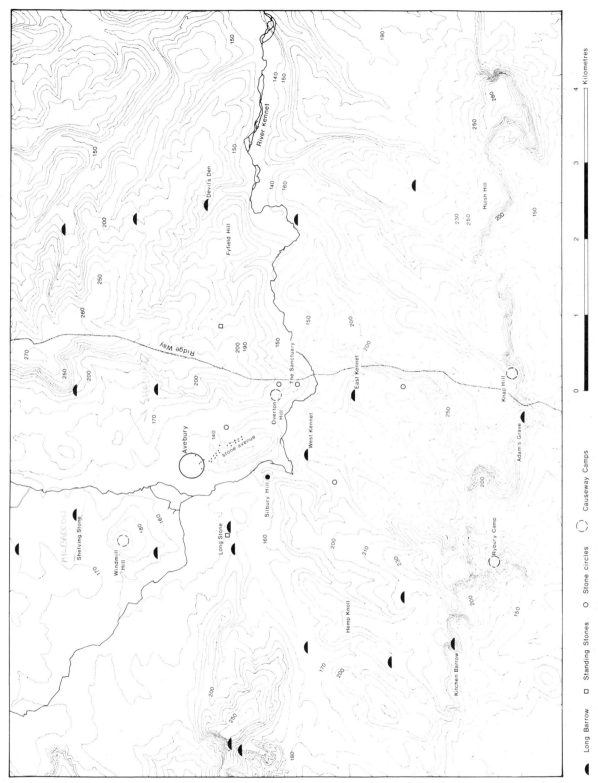

22 *Map of the Neolithic monuments of Avebury.*

dating from as early as 3400 bc (4350 BC) but most barrows and enclosures dating from after *c*.3000 bc (3710 BC). It was nearly another thousand years before the henges, avenues and great ceremonial landscapes of the later Neolithic period were in use. The evolution of the different types of Neolithic monument and structure over the 2000-year period that is the subject of this book relates to changes which were both technological and social.

As these transformations were happening, ceremonial and religious activities changed and these changes were reflected in the type and arrangement of the ceremonial monuments that were currently in use.

Long barrows

The most numerous of the early monuments that make up the Neolithic landscape are the long barrows. These now number a few hundred, but must once have been present in their thousands throughout Britain. They vary in construction and size, but are all fundamentally repositories for the remains of the dead. There are a few exceptions, such as South Street long barrow in Avebury, which contained no human bones at all.

The first long barrows (23) were initially quite modest structures, intended to house the bodies of the pioneering ancestors who first settled in the Avebury area. Access to the tombs for burial was probably based on family links, rather than on earned status. But within a few generations of the barrows being built, new, perhaps competitive, aims dominated the design and subsequent use of the tombs. Far from being modest, the barrows, especially in the Avebury area, became larger and more prominent in the landscape, and contained chambers within which only carefully-selected individuals were buried. Selection may have been through age, sex, clan membership, and perhaps later on, through social status. The arrangement of the chambers within the larger tombs may also have been symbolic in some way. The tombs were labour-intensive in construction to an extent quite unparalleled by contemporary building work. The excavation of the ditches and the piling up of chalk, soil and rubble involved quite massive investments of labour, and was not done overnight. However, in comparison to the later monuments the effort invested even in these barrows was still modest, and may be a fair reflection of the sum total of

23 *Aerial view of the West Kennet long barrow before excavation and restoration. Note that all the stones of the facade are flat on the ground.*

the type of labour investment available in the earlier part of the Neolithic period, before much land was cleared, and before the new agricultural economy could be relied upon to allow time away from work on husbandry.

The construction of these enduring and highly visible mausolea gave the living communities a link with their past ancestors, and in turn a link to those ancestors' claim to, or ownership of, the land around them. Thus as each generation lived, died and was buried in the family tombs, the link with, and indeed the ownership of the past, was handed on. We can see parallels to this more recently in parish churches, where family tombs, perhaps with a marble figure, coat of arms, iron railings or decorated slab, and the ubiquitous inscription, are part of a tradition which goes back to these ancient communities of the long barrows.

The way such barrows were built varies across Britain according to the local geology. In the chalklands, the earthen barrow with chalk and flint rubble at the core is most usual. In areas like Avebury, where there was local stone available, there was a mix of materials, resulting in the chalk, sarsen and earth barrow, with local sarsen stone used for the entrance and chambers, as well as imported oolitic limestone brought from a distance of some 10–15 miles (16–24 km). In the west of England and

Wales the barrow tradition is dominated by more substantial constructions, the chamber tombs and the passage graves; these used large megalithic stones with uprights supporting huge capstones, arranged as long passages with chambers opening from them. The whole structure was then covered with stones and soil, much as at West Kennet. In the highland area, large stones seem to have been rejected in favour of smaller stones, which were formed into cairns of roughly oval shape. Some of these have internal chambers, but soil was rarely used to cover the structures, since it was usually too sparse to collect on the rocky hillsides.

Causewayed enclosures

The long barrows, although communal in function, were quite possibly constructed piecemeal for family or kinship groups. Causewayed enclosures, on the other hand, the next component added to the landscape, involved a long-term investment of time and effort, and were undoubtedly the combined work of many families or lineage groups over a sustained period of time. Whereas the barrows followed a few clear patterns of design and had an obvious function, the enclosures did not. Each was different, and may have had a multitude of functions. They followed no specific design, and their construction and arrangement may have been directed by an individual or by a small select group of influential people, who organized the digging of the ditches and the activities that were practised within the area encircled. The 50 or so causewayed enclosure sites that are known in southern and central England are only the relatively well-preserved survivors of what must once have been many more.

It is not possible to be certain in each case which was the principal intended function at the time of construction. Each of the enclosures which have been investigated archaeologically has provided differing, and often enigmatic evidence for the activities that went on in them. Some were clearly used as enclosures for groups of smaller structures or huts, and may have been temporary camps or even settlements. One traditional interpretation has been that the enclosures served as corrals in which cattle, sheep and pigs would have been kept, perhaps for culling, trading or eating. It is certainly true that most causewayed sites have produced great quantities of animal bones. Many sites have also produced materials and tools which are alien to the immediate area of the enclosure, and therefore one interpretation of the sites has been that they were used as markets and meeting places for a sparsely spread population in the surrounding area. Some of the chalk downland enclosure sites, such as Windmill Hill, were located near flint mines or good flint sources, and have produced great quantities of flint tools and waste material, suggesting that a flint knapping industry might have been located there.

Most causewayed enclosures have produced evidence for human burials, often scattered in the bottom of the surrounding enclosure ditches, along with animal skeletons and food and domestic refuse. A few sites have offered evidence that the banks built around the sites may have been revetted with wooden palisades, and this may have been defensive in function. Thus the evidence is varied and difficult to interpret. No one site seems to have had a single function, and we should regard the causewayed enclosures as the first major composite sites, with multiple and probably changing functions throughout their long span of use.

Henges and other circular constructions

Whilst the causewayed enclosures were in their heyday of use around 3000 BC (2350 bc), other smaller, exclusively ceremonial, sites began to appear in the landscape. These were the first henges and circular buildings, which were usually located close to the causewayed sites. The low bank and ditch of Stonehenge and its first settings of stones, together with the circular building of the Sanctuary, were two of the first such structures to appear in Wessex. It was to be several centuries before these new ceremonial sites took over the role of the causewayed enclosure sites altogether.

By the time Silbury Hill was built, around 2700 BC (2150 bc), the largest man-made mound in Europe, the organization and control of society had reached a new level. Silbury Hill was the most labour intensive piece of construction in Neolithic Britain; it has been calculated that it would have taken 800 men ten years to complete, and that is if they worked on it all the year round. Such a calculation takes no account of the agricultural needs of a fairly simple society, where each individual probably still needed to work quite hard to produce food for himself, so the real manpower figures

24 *Aerial view of the West Kennet pit enclosure, one of the less understood monuments of Avebury*

the construction of the circles indicate that similarly large numbers of people were involved for considerable lengths of time, in what was clearly intended as a public monument. The building of the henges and stone circles in the later Neolithic period represented the last corporate building works until the much later construction of the Iron Age hillforts, some 1500 years later. Clearly social organization had developed a high level of either cooperative labour or, more likely, of totalitarian control of the labour force in the later centuries of the Neolithic period, reaching its apex at Avebury.

The structure of Neolithic society

Ideas about Neolithic society have changed very much over the last few years. The view of primitive man as hairy, ape-like creatures clad in skins is no longer accepted. Current expert opinion, based on a combination of archaeological evidence, and on ethnographic parallels from non-westernized parts of the world, suggests that the Neolithic people lived in a comparatively sophisticated society, and were physically no different from ourselves. Although the archaeological evidence is not precise, it is believed that Neolithic people dressed in garments made from well-cured animal skins, woven linen and wool, perhaps with elaborate embroidery, painted patterns and other decoration. Like some of the more remote communities in Africa, Asia, Oceania and central and south America today, they probably had elaborate hairstyles, and perhaps indulged in body painting and tattoos.

The main preoccupation of many archaeologists is to understand the social organization of ancient communities. There is no surviving written history, and mere study of the individuals found in burial mounds cannot provide a full picture of how society was organized, or tell us which people had power over the rest. Indeed, we cannot really say whether men or women were in control, or whether there was an elected chief, or a family or tribal leader. There may have been a small group of elderly people representing each family, who decided how things were to be organized, or again, society may have been completely egalitarian, or self-ruling. The building of the great

involved can only be guessed at. The clear design of Silbury, and the control that was exerted over the construction of the monument, suggest that the social structure had changed considerably from the apparently egalitarian lineages of the earlier Neolithic period, to one which was directed from the top, perhaps even by an emerging tribal or clan chief and his family.

By the middle of the third millennium BC, henges began to take a dominant role in the landscape of Neolithic centres. Henges were enclosure sites, similar in concept to the causewayed enclosures, except that the ditches were deeper and more continuous, with only one to four causewayed entrances. A high bank around the ditch, usually inside, but sometimes outside (like Avebury), formed an impressive boundary to the site, within which were circular buildings, settings of wooden posts, and stone and wooden circles. These sites were apparently used exclusively for non-domestic purposes, and there is no evidence that animals were kept in them, or that there were any domestic dwellings.

The building of the Avebury henge suggests that the establishment of more centralized control over building works, apparent at Silbury, had become further refined. The excavation of the massive ditches and the collection and erection of the vast sarsen stones used in

25 *Reconstruction of the interior of a Neolithic house (Judith Dobie).*

monuments during the middle and later Neolithic period does indicate, however, that someone, or some sector of society, was able to organize large groups of workers to design and construct the great ceremonial monuments. Even if the edifices were the result of massive communal effort, someone had to decide when, where and how these complex and technically innovative structures were to be built. One of the main problems in the archaeology of the Neolithic period in Britain is the lack of good settlement evidence, for although we know of

many sites from superficial flint scatters, few actual settlements have been found or excavated. Without the evidence of villages and of individual houses, with their rubbish heaps and working areas, interpretation of domestic life is difficult. Were such sites to be found in the Avebury area of elsewhere, it might be possible to discover how large settlements were and suggest the size of their populations, besides gaining a greater understanding of their economies and social organization.

Drawing upon social anthropology, however, useful parallels can be found in the formation and workings of simple societies in other parts

26 *Diagram of a segmentary lineage system over four generations, each segment having its own territory adjacent to its brothers (after Bohannan – The Expansion and Migration of the Tiv).*

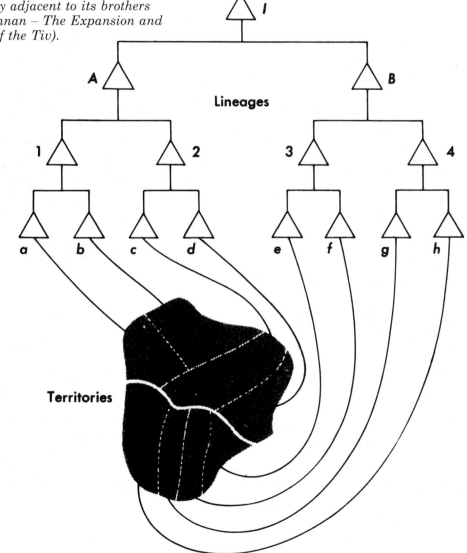

44

of the world. Primitive farming groups are usually organized into family groups, which in turn derive their identity from their lineage or tribe. Common ancestors, who may be real or mythical in origin, are used to link otherwise unrelated people together, so that they regard themselves a members of one kin. Farming communities need to maintain their claim to their land, since they regard the investment of labour in the past as their claim to the future possession of it, and the common ancestors who owned and farmed the land have thus established the right of the present generation to hold it in their turn.

There has been much speculation on how the monument society evolved in prehistoric Wessex. It has been suggested that Neolithic

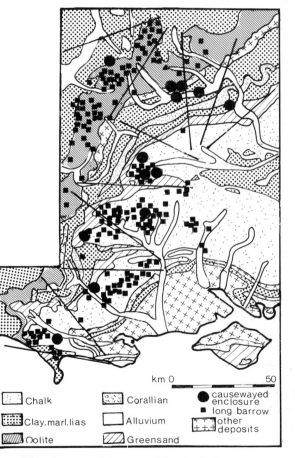

27 *Sketch map of the possible Neolithic territories in Wessex, showing Neolithic monuments in relation to geology (after Barker and Webley 1978).*

people were organized into several lineage segments, all ultimately derived from a common ancestor, which held territories adjoining each other (26). These lineage segments were not ranked, nor did they have any continuous organizational role. Instead, each one was bound by alliances with the other groups, which alliances were only activated if there was conflict between any of them. At times of stress when there was strife with neighbouring groups, or during famine, then a temporary chief or leader might emerge. One of the features of the segmentary lineages found in nineteenth-century Africa, is that they were expansionist and tended to spread their territories outwards, though only into areas occupied by non-lineage groups; clearly this was because they were bound to respect the boundaries of their lineage 'brothers'.

In an attempt to interpret the landscape of Neolithic Wessex, elaborate theories have been constructed using the causewayed enclosures, the long barrows, and the henges as the central points of individual territories, as well as identifying barrows supposedly sited as territorial markers along their boundaries. Environmentally, too, it is possible to divide the landscape of Wessex quite convincingly into numerous territories (27), each with some lowland or valley bottom, hillslope and upland, thus providing each one with its share of essential agricultural land types. Some researchers have used the geological and soil evidence in this way as a basis for defining possible prehistoric territories.

By the later Neolithic period, we may conclude that the segmentary lineage system of the fourth and early third millennium BC had been replaced by a much more centralized political system, that of a clan, in which a social structure that supported a chiefdom emerged. This was a system of inherited power based on descent from a dominant lineage. Such a system could have come about because various segmentary lineages had merged, or because one segment had broken away from the dominant lineage. A changing economic and social environment might have resulted in one powerful individual taking political control over the entire community.

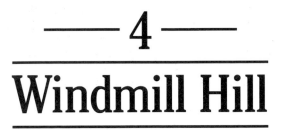

4

Windmill Hill

The site in the Neolithic period

Windmill Hill at Avebury (28) is the 'type site' for the Neolithic causewayed 'camp' or enclosure. Its special characteristics were first recognised over sixty years ago and it was one of the first Neolithic 'settlement' sites to be extensively researched. The significance of the

28 *Aerial view of Windmill Hill, taken soon after the excavations, with the causewayed ditches clearly showing.*

causewayed enclosure sites has been discussed previously, and my intention here is to describe Windmill Hill in its Neolithic context, and to discuss its role as one of the sites which have revolutionized our knowledge and interpretation of the remote period to which it belongs.

Windmill Hill is the largest of all the known causewayed enclosure sites in Britain. The three concentric rings of ditches enclose a total area of about 21 acres (9 ha), the outer ditch

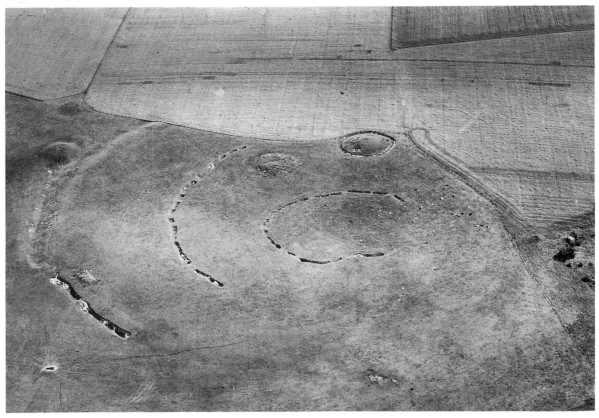

varying from 1000 to 1270 ft (304 m–387 m) in diameter. It is located north-west of Avebury, on the side of the summit of the hill that bears the site's name, at a height of 630–643 ft (192–8 m) above sea level. The hilltop is enclosed by three concentric rings of ditches. None of these are continuous, being broken at intervals by causeways or unexcavated 'bridges' of chalk. The excavated contents of the ditches were deposited as banks on the inner edge of each ditch, thus emphasizing the depth of the ditch. The outer ditch was the deepest of the three, and reached a maximum of 9 ft 6 in (2.74 m) in places, although 7 ft (2.13 m) was the average depth. The middle ditch reached an average of 4.6 ft (1.37 m) and the inner ditch an average of only 3.1 ft (.94 m). The banks were revetted with wooden posts to prevent the chalk collapsing back into the ditch.

The regular plan of Windmill Hill is typical of the more complex causewayed enclosure sites. Some sites, such as Whitesheet Hill and Rybury Hill on the scarp above the Vale of Pewsey, have only one ring of ditches; this is also the case with several others elsewhere, including Orsett (Essex) and Maiden Castle (Dorset). Others have two rings of ditches, including Robin Hood's Ball near Stonehenge and Coombe Hill (Sussex). More complex sites include the enclosure site on Overton Hill (near Avebury); Whitehawk Hill (Wiltshire); the Trundle (West Sussex); and the three or four separate enclosures that make up the complex on Hambledon Hill (Dorset). New sites of this type continue to come to light through the use of aerial photography, and whereas two decades ago sites were mostly known from the chalk downland of southern England, they have now been recognized on the gravel terraces of lowland valleys and in the wetlands of the Cambridgeshire fenland. Some sites, such as Crickley Hill (Gloucestershire), on the high limestone scarp edge of the Cotswolds near Cheltenham, appear to be located on sites which offered the maximum natural protection. Indeed, the discovery of great numbers of arrowheads during recent excavations there suggests that the site had a partly defensive function. Sites of a similar date, but which are not surrounded by causewayed ditches, include some which are clearly defensive in nature with high banks around them, such as Hembury Hill in Devon. Excavations there showed that the site had actually been attacked, since arrowheads, burnt structures and the remains of human bodies were found in great numbers.

A more detailed examination of Windmill Hill gives some clearer indications of how these enclosures were used, and how their original functions may have altered in the course of their existence. The first farmers in Britain appear to have cleared woodland, built settlements, constructed long barrows and cultivated the landscape from about 4375 BC (3500 bc). It was nearly 500 years later that the enclosure sites were constructed. At Windmill Hill, evidence in the form of occasional Palaeolithic and Mesolithic flint tools suggests that earlier hunting groups visited the hilltop. In the period following the last Ice Age, Windmill Hill was probably covered with the indigenous mixed oak woodlands that typified the environment of southern England – beech, elm, ash, lime, hazel and other trees and fruit bushes – growing from an undisturbed forest soil, built up over thousands of years.

Although so many new sites have been identified in the lowlands of southern Britain, the greatest concentration of causewayed sites recognized to date are on the chalk Downs and the Cotswolds in the south and west Midlands. Light, well-drained soils offered the highest yields for cereal agriculture. These were mainly intermediate soils from the rich clay or 'cornbrash'; the greensands at the fringes of the chalk and limestone hills and corallian ridges; and the alluvial soils in the valleys of the Downs. These were the areas that had previously carried relatively open woodland, and were thus the most easily cleared and cultivated.

Windmill Hill is located on a pronounced eminence above two small streams (the Winterbourns) flowing on the east and west sides, above the larger headwater valley of the Kennett. This situation offered three essential natural elements for the foundation of a site that was to become the regional centre for over a thousand years: these were the lightly wooded slopes of the hill above the streams, easily cleared and drained, with rich alluvial soils suitable for cereal agriculture; springs and seasonal streams, providing water; and finally a prominent hilltop site commanding views in all directions over the surrounding wooded country. Other factors which helped determine its siting were probably the nearby Ridgeway path; easy access to both the Kennett and

Thames valleys; local sources of good flint for toolmaking; and perhaps most fundamental of all, a well-established claim to the territory by the local Neolithic community who had constructed several long barrows in the area in the preceding centuries. The site was located at a natural junction between high downland and the river valleys, between different territorial regions. As in the case of certain other causewayed sites, this choice of location may have been intended to bring different groups together for the performance of various activities there.

Study of the siting of Neolithic causewayed sites has suggested that each was probably located in a self-contained geographical territory (27). The communities using the causewayed sites were engaged in mixed cereal cultivation and stock-rearing. These had differing requirements: the cereals needed light, well-drained soils, while the animals (cows, pigs, sheep, and goats) required grazing throughout the year. Thus each Neolithic community needed a territory that provided several types of landscape. From studies of the prehistoric grain produced by the Windmill Hill community, six-rowed and naked barley were probably the most common cereal, which flourished on the downland slopes and in the chalk valleys. Emmer, bread and einkorn wheats, flax and spelt (all primitive cereal types) were also grown in varying quantities. No fields survive from the Neolithic period, but areas of cultivation, perhaps in strips or small plots, were doubtless clearly defined with fences or hedges to prevent animals straying over them.

A permanent settlement was probably located nearby, perhaps along the stream terraces. We know very little about these small everyday living sites, since archaeological exploration has failed to locate any coherent traces of them. Small amounts of flint, pot and bone are often encountered when fieldwork is done, and occasionally pits and hearths also come to light in excavation. However, in the Avebury area there is no clear evidence yet to point to where the earlier Neolithic farmers actually lived. Dense scatters of domestic flint tools and waste flakes have been found in the fields adjoining the henge at Avebury, and on the lower slopes of Windmill Hill, suggesting the possible presence of former settlements. The Kennett valley and its tributary streams all look suitable for small agricultural plots with

river terraces and gentle slopes above the streams suitable for settlement.

We can therefore postulate a possible landscape: green watermeadows in the bottom of the valleys, with small hamlets of thatched huts made of wattle and daub on the first terrace above. The settlements may have been almost continuous villages in some areas, with animal pens, haystacks, small granaries, pits and extensive areas of rotting domestic rubbish, the smell drifting and mingling with animal odours above the hamlets. On the slightly higher slopes there may have been small fenced-in fields or allotments of various cereals and herbs. Beyond, there would have been stands of large forest trees, relics of the old forest, surrounded by rough grassland with bushes, areas of thin woodland, and some patches of heath and bracken. Leading up to the higher Downs, there might have been wide well-trodden tracks, along which the animals were driven to more distant grazing land.

In such a landscape, Windmill Hill (28) would have been the dominating feature. White chalk banks, freshly dug from the surrounding ditches, must have stood out clearly, as would the open nature of the hilltop in comparison to the scrubby profiles of the surrounding country. This effect may have been deliberately achieved. As the largest man-made edifice in the landscape, Windmill Hill could be seen for miles, and would draw surrounding communities to the festivals and activities that periodically broke the monotony of agricultural life. The enclosure also provided a refuge in time of trouble within its high revetted banks.

Some more recent evidence adds further detail to the picture. Aerial photography has identified another causewayed enclosure only 2 miles (3 km) from Windmill Hill, on the southern flank of Overton Hill, immediately above the line of the West Kennet Avenue. This site has three ditches (31), and although only a portion of it is visible, it seems that it may eventually be found to have been as large as Windmill Hill. Unfortunately the site has not yet been investigated, and there is no information on its dating or the contents of the ditches. Its proximity to the Windmill Hill site – the largest of its type – is difficult to explain. When more is known about the site, it may suggest why the Avebury area became a supremely important Neolithic centre, since the existence of two such large sites in close proximity

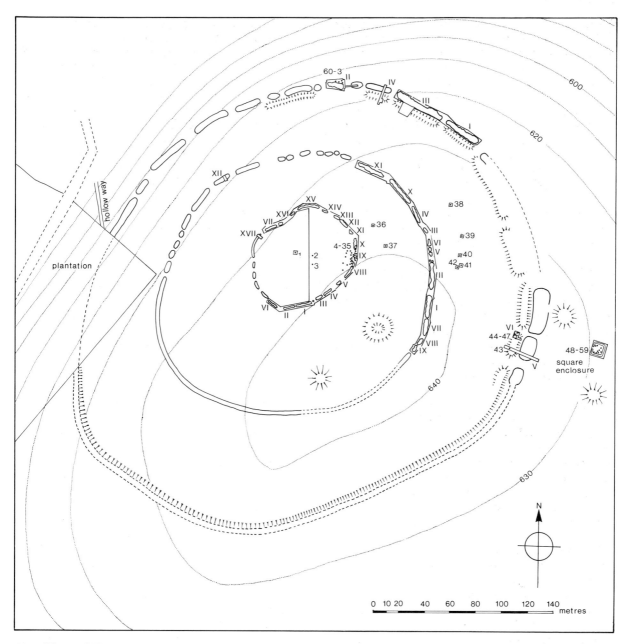

29 *Plan of Windmill Hill after Keiller's excavations (1925–9).*

promises to be unique in Britain.

The archaeological evidence from Windmill Hill is some of the best so far studied, since relatively few other causewayed sites have been so extensively investigated. Excavations took place between 1925–29, 1936, and 1957–8, and again in 1988, and have afforded detailed evidence about the pre-enclosure settlement, the enclosure itself, the use to which it was put and the continuity of use on the hilltop.

People appear to have inhabited the hilltop before the three concentric rings of ditches were dug. A cluster of 32 small pits on the east side of the inner ditch were excavated and then filled, some with worked flint, pot and local sarsen stone (**32a**). They were probably used for storing grain or foods, and were filled in soon after they went out of use. The upcast banks formed from the fill of the ditches which

49

30 *The ditches of Windmill Hill were dug in separate sections leaving chalk causeways between each section. Here the cuttings VI and V of the middle ditch show the variable depth of each section.*

31 *Aerial view of the causewayed enclosure on Overton Hill. The road on the left of the picture follows the Avenue to Avebury (Royal Commission on Historical Monuments).*

surrounded the causewayed enclosure covered and sealed the soil beneath them. Here more traces of settlement debris were found, together with post-built structures, perhaps huts; a stone-ringed hearth; and other groups of post holes or pits, some of which had daub linings, and others which had linings of pure brown clay (**32b**). Within some of the pits were objects that might have been placed there symbolically,

including a piece of oolitic limestone from several miles away, a leaf-shaped flint flake, flint scrapers, cores and flakes, and animal bone. Environmental evidence from soil buried under the later Neolithic banks indicated that the whole area had been cultivated, and the pollen grains preserved in the soil were from cereals, and from weeds normally associated with cornfields. The radio-carbon date for this early occupation was 3700 BC (2960 bc), which suggests that this early settlement was a little later than the Horslip Long barrow on the slopes of Windmill Hill.

Lower down on the eastern slope of the hill, just outside the position later occupied by the

51

32b *The pits, excavated by Keiller.*

32a *Plan of pits from the early pre-enclosure occupation of Windmill Hill around the inner ditch.*

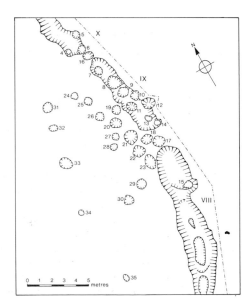

outer ditch, was an unusual square structure, made up of excavated gullies around the edge, and containing 12 pits very similar to the group of 32 higher up (**33**). All but two of these also contained objects, including flints, pottery, bone, pieces of stone and sarsen, and imported oolitic limestone. It is possible to reconstruct the enclosure as a square building of substantial posts surrounded with a wattle and daub wall, with the wattle posts bedded into the gully trenches. The structure has some parallels with mortuary houses from other Neolithic sites where structures apparently dedicated to funerary use contained large quantities of human remains. In some instances these structures were then incorporated with long barrows, as

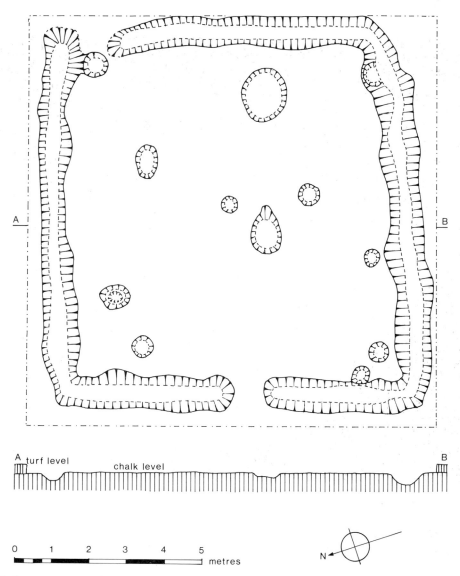

A turf level   chalk level   B

0   1   2   3   4   5
                        metres   N

33 *Plan of the square enclosure on Windmill Hill.*

at Fussell's Lodge (Berkshire), and Nutbane (Hampshire).

All the constructions so far described appear, as already mentioned, to have predated the excavation of the banks and ditches of the causewayed enclosure. These were excavated some time before 3400 BC (2580 bc), but it is not known if they were all dug and completed at one time or in a sequence. It has been suggested that the interrupted character of the ditches, with the rough chalk causeways left between them, may have resulted from the employment of different gangs of workers. It is probable that the massive effort of digging the three

ditches happened rather spasmodically, in slack periods of the agricultural year, and that it was undertaken by several different local lineage groups, each collaborating in stretches on the construction of the community earthwork. Thus each small section might have been the work of a few people. It has been estimated that 62–64,000 man-hours went into the construction of the site, perhaps over several years, as the successive ditches were added.

Since the outer ditch was the deepest, it probably had the highest bank, mounded up on its inner edge. Although most of these banks have now disappeared, either through silting back into the ditch or from more recent ploughing, traces of the buried turf levels have been located by excavation. It seems that the banks

53

34 *Animal and human bones lay in discrete clusters along the base of the excavated ditches, representing special deposits of feasts, sacrifices and burials.*

were probably more or less continuous, and may have been supported by wooden revetments of posts driven through them. Recent excavations at Hambledon Hill (Dorset) have suggested that the banks may have been defensive in purpose. The ditches were certainly used at Windmill Hill for disposing of large quantities of domestic material including animal bones and human bodies (**34**). There were also two complete child skeletons, and numerous other skeletal fragments. One child was buried in the shallowest part of the outer ditch (**35**) in close proximity to a young pig and goat (**36a,c**). A complete dog (**36b**) was found in the middle ditch, and another child in the inner ditch. All had been buried intentionally, and may have been placed

in such a way that they had ritual significance.

At Hambledon Hill, there were several different and quite independent enclosures and associated ditches on different elevations of the very large hilltop. Some were filled with normal domestic rubbish, but others had clearly symbolic materials deposited along the base. The main inner ditch of the Stepleton enclosure had abnormally high quantities of domestic material deliberately buried with human remains. Along an area forming 20 per cent of the base of the ditch were some 70 human skulls, all placed with care, presumably as part of a symbolic act, perhaps dedicating the site to the dead. Similar arrangements of human bones may once have adorned the entrances into the enclosure at Windmill Hill, being placed on mortuary platforms, totem poles or in buildings on the site during a period when death rituals may have been the dominant activity on the site. These rituals seem to have been associated with curious chalk carvings representing

35 *A child burial was found at the base of one ditch, and was removed complete for display in the Avebury Museum. The child had suffered from water on the brain, or hydrocephalous, leaving the skull much enlarged.*

37 *A chalk carving, perhaps phallic, found in the ditches of Windmill Hill. These objects may have had a ceremonial or ritual purpose.*

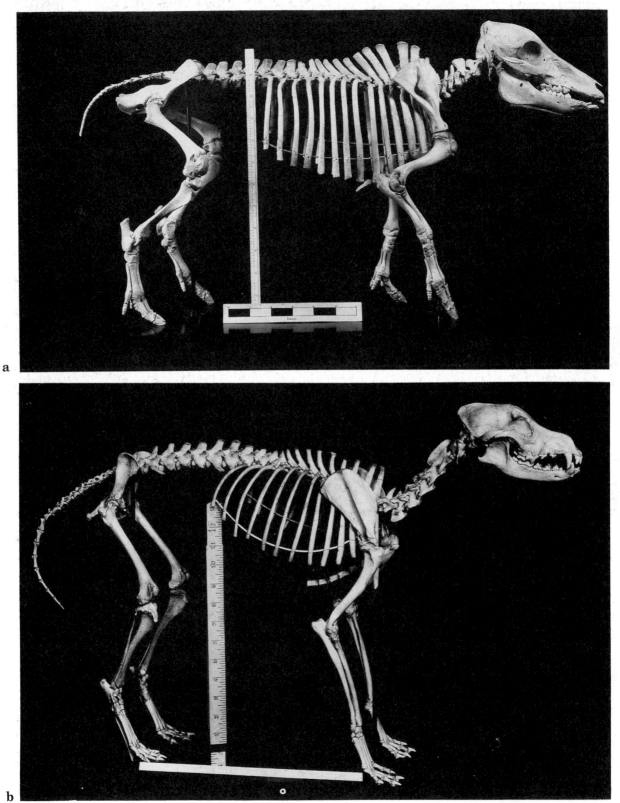

a

b

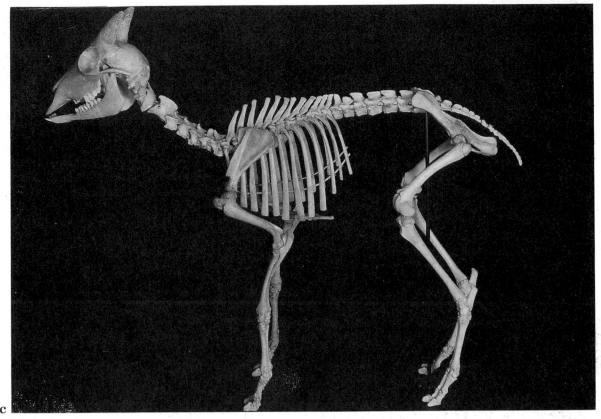

c

36 *Complete animal skeletons were sometimes found in the Windmill Hill ditches, perhaps buried as special offerings:*
(a) young pig; (b) dog; (c) young sheep/goat.

female figurines, chalk balls and phalli (**37**).

At Windmill Hill it is possible that the square building outside the main enclosures may have been constructed as a mortuary house, where the dead were laid, perhaps to the accompaniment of special rituals, processions and the words of the local 'wise man' or his equivalent (**colour plate 1**). Anthropological research from other parts of the world suggests that the bodies may have been left until the flesh had rotted from the bones. Then the bones may have been collected up, with certain bones such as the skulls and long bones being kept for special rituals on Windmill Hill, and the rest either scattered in the causewayed ditches (see **34**) or taken to the long barrows to join the bones of the ancestors. The Stepleton enclosure on Hambledon Hill may have been used almost solely for similar death rituals. It has been suggested that the whole area must have been

a stinking morgue, with corpses in varying states of disintegration littering the area. Such practices still occur today in Nepal and other remote places.

The Windmill Hill causewayed site may also have been the scene of less unappealing activities, including the herding together and then the selection and slaughter of farm animals, followed by feasting. The quantity of animal bone from Windmill Hill is so great that it has led to the suggestion that the feasting may have had a ceremonial or ritual significance. Cattle, pigs and sheep, together with occasional deer, horses and hares, were slaughtered and eaten, and their remains were buried alongside the human remains in the ditches.

Perhaps in conjunction with the feasts, other, more commercial activities also took place. The enormous quantities of well-made pottery, much apparently not native to the Avebury area, together with polished axes from stone sources throughout the British Isles, and vast numbers of finely made flint tools, suggest that the site also acted as a centre for the exchange of goods, as a market. In comparison with other contemporary Neolithic sites, Windmill Hill has

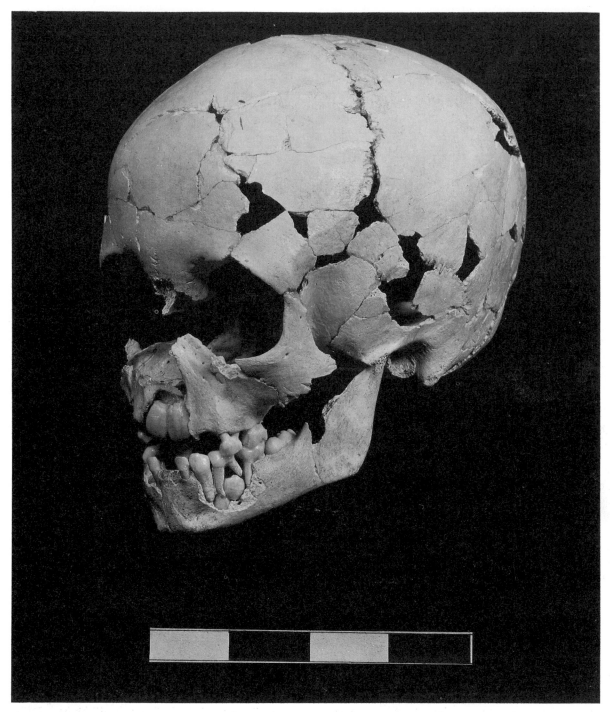

38 *Human skulls were found in the ditches of Windmill Hill, often not associated with other parts of the skeleton. They may have been used in special ceremonies using skulls and long bones, and have been taken from the long barrows for this purpose.*

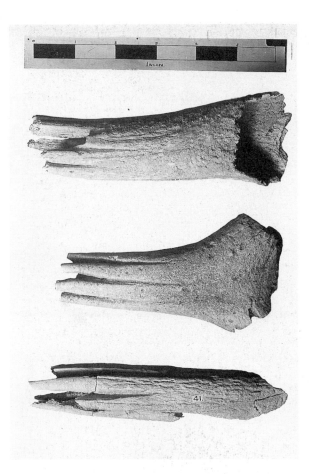

39 *Antler combs were one of the more unusual classes of artefact found on Windmill Hill, and were perhaps used for weaving cloth.*

a far greater variety of different pottery styles and non-local stone objects. Although we cannot be certain what took place on Windmill Hill, all the evidence suggests that the site acted as a gathering place when both local populations, and groups from more distant areas, may well have congregated for special events, when animals were exchanged and flints, axes and pots were traded, as well as craft produce and more perishable goods, like leather, baskets, dried foods, special herbs, carved wood and bone objects, antler combs (**39**), paints and ochre. Windmill Hill, together with its twin site on Overton Hill, seems therefore to have had a multiplicity of functions, perhaps organized seasonally, with festivals and markets in the summer, and the rituals of death and burial being celebrated during other parts of the year.

Like other enclosure sites, Windmill Hill was probably also used as a settlement for much of its life, as it had been before the enclosure was constructed. The quantities of domestic rubbish, flint knapping debris, post holes and hearths all suggest a substantial community. The usual interpretation of causewayed enclosures has been that they were settlements, but it is possible that they were inhabited for only a relatively short period of time. It may be that the groups who settled within the enclosure were of particularly high status or connected with specific activities, such as organizing the ceremonials and religious life of the whole community.

Subsequent history of the site

Windmill Hill's role as a focal point in the Avebury area continued throughout the Neolithic period and even into the earlier Bronze Age, in the early centuries of the second millennium BC. Evidence in the form of new types of pottery (**41**) and stone tools (**42**) demonstrates that whilst the types of activities on the hill changed, the importance of the site was undiminished. Bones and rubbish were no longer placed in the now silted ditches of the site, and the rubbish of earlier centuries was completely buried. The site appears to have become less frequented during the later centuries of the Neolithic period (in the late third millennium BC) with only sporadic deposits of pottery and bone finding their way into the ditches. This was almost certainly because the causewayed site had all but been replaced in importance by the new henge at Avebury, less than one mile away.

The pottery used by the Neolithic farmers of Avebury changed gradually during the 1500 years or so that Windmill Hill retained importance. Initially, plain, round-based pots of varying sizes made up the bulk of vessels, with only a few of them showing any signs of decoration (**40**). These pots had small handles, decorative knobs and lugs for suspending the pots from strings, and were probably used for domestic cooking and storage of food, cereals and water. In use alongside these local pots were some imported from as far away as Devon and East Anglia. These may have been exchanged or have been presented as gifts. In particular, Hembury pottery, Mildenhall, Abingdon and Whitehawk types have been found. Hembury pottery was plain and similar to the Windmill Hill pottery, but the others were

40 *Sketch of Windmill Hill pottery. The small lugs were used for suspending the vessels for storage and cooking (Judith Dobie).*

highly decorated and had more interesting shapes. In the later phases of Windmill Hill, decorated pottery became more frequent, with incised Peterborough types, and Grooved ware pottery. In the final phases of the Neolithic period, Beaker pottery also appeared (see **56**). Many of the more decorated pottery types have been identified more with ceremonial than domestic sites, and it is tempting to interpret the presence of such types of pottery on Windmill Hill with special types of feasting and drinking, perhaps with the introduction of alcoholic drinks like mead and ale. Flint working was also carried out on the hill (**42**).

From the end of the third millennium BC, Windmill Hill seems to have been largely abandoned. But it seems likely that a folk memory of the former importance of the site lived on since the summit of the hill became the focus of a Bronze Age cemetery. The remains of the great tumuli can still be seen dominating the skyline. Unfortunately most of the burial mounds have been excavated long ago, so that we have little information about the structure or contents of the barrows. In 1936 Alexander Keiller opened up one barrow where rabbits had disturbed an intact burial urn (now to be seen in the Keiller Museum in Avebury) (**44**). It is interesting to note that the Overton Hill enclosure site is also dominated by huge round barrows, some of them covered by trees.

Later, in the Roman period, Windmill Hill was probably deserted. On the lower southern flanks a large Roman villa was built, and pottery of Roman date has been found scattered thinly over the hill, perhaps being transported there in household and farmyard manure by Roman farmers.

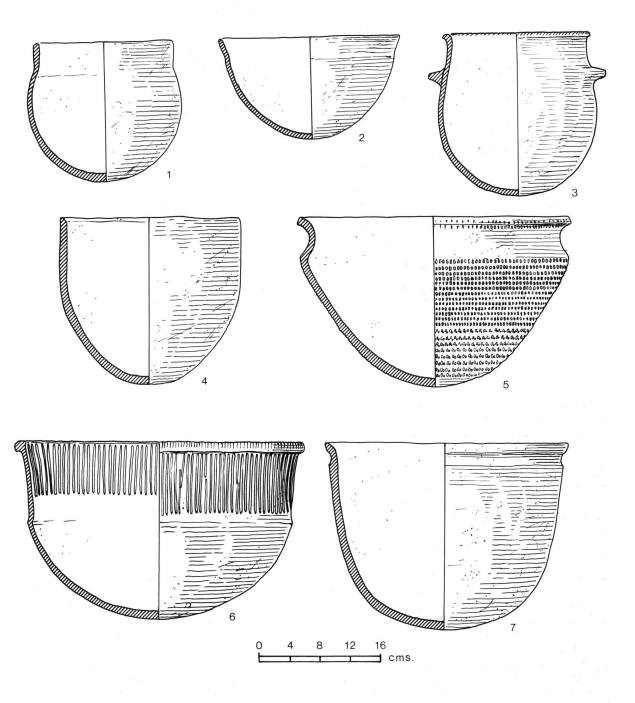

41 *Windmill Hill pottery from Windmill Hill
(after Smith 1965).*

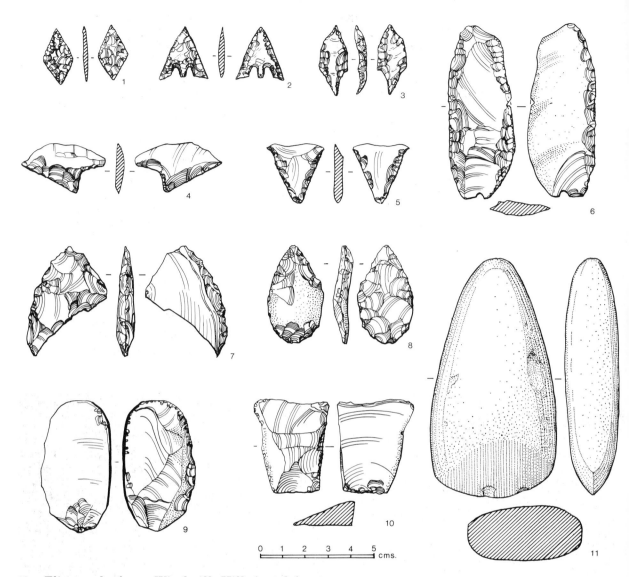

0 1 2 3 4 5 cms.

42 *Flint tools from Windmill Hill (top left to bottom right): triangular arrowhead; leaf-shaped arrowhead; awl; double-sided scraper; transverse of petit-tranchet arrowheads × 2; broken laurel leaf-knife; laurel leaf knife; polished edge knife; sickle flint; polished axe (after Smith 1965).*

Related local sites

About 4 miles (6.4 km) south of Avebury, Knap Hill (**45**) on the edge of the chalk escarpment is a spectacular site, commanding views over Pewsey Vale. Excavations have not produced such extensive data as Windmill Hill, however, but the functions of the site may have been similar if on a much more modest scale. The presence of the impressive long barrow of Adam's Grave nearby and the varied resources available within the likely territory of the causewayed site are comparable to those of Windmill Hill. It probably functioned as the secondary centre for the local Neolithic groups

43 *Sketch of Neolithic flint knappers at work (Judith Dobie).*

44 *Bronze Age burial urn uncovered by rabbits on the side of a barrow on Windmill Hill.*

45 *Knap Hill causewayed enclosure from the air.*

farming the fertile Pewsey Vale, and like Windmill Hill, was succeeded by a massive henge monument, Avebury in the case of Windmill Hill and Marden in relation to Knap Hill.

Further south, on Salisbury Plain, the causewayed site of Robin Hood's Ball, now within the army artillery ranges, formed a similar complex, but without the dramatic variation of geography and resources demonstrated by the north Wiltshire locations. There were several Neolithic long barrows within the projected territory, as well as two later henge monuments, Stonehenge and Durrington Walls-Woodhenge. On the same escarpment as Knap Hill is the site of Rybury Camp. This is a small causewayed enclosure of similar date to Windmill Hill.

The archaeology of the site:
the work of Kendall, Gray and Keiller

The Neolithic importance of Windmill Hill was only recognized earlier this century. An elderly clergyman, the Reverend Kendall, vicar of Winterbourne Monkton, regularly pursued his passion for flint collecting on the summit of Windmill Hill, immediately to the south of his parish. The hill had long been known as one of the best flint-hunting areas, and over the years, Kendall picked up literally thousands of flint tools, arrowheads and flint waste in the

ploughed fields. One day, however, he found some Neolithic pottery which was unlike anything he had previously encountered. Soon, the site became well known as one of the very few sites in England producing Neolithic pottery from what appeared to be a settlement.

After the First World War, advances in technology threatened the site, when Marconi the wireless pioneer planned to build a relay station on the summit of the hill. The distinguished Ordnance Survey archaeologist O. G. S. Crawford, heard of the scheme, and having only recently mapped the presence of rare Neolithic pottery on the site, he alerted archaeological colleagues and started a campaign to save the site. Crawford's most influential ally was his friend Alexander Keiller, an amateur archaeologist and heir of the Dundee marmalade firm. Crawford and Keiller in 1924 researched and wrote *Wessex from the Air*, a novel subject at the time, and they had begun to recognize the full potential of the splendid prehistoric sites of Wessex. With Crawford's help, Keiller organized a campaign against Marconi's plans, with publicity and support from influential people. Before long, Marconi changed their minds about the site, and Windmill Hill was saved. Keiller bought the hilltop himself in 1924, so that it would never be threatened again. Kendall, the original discoverer of the site, acted as local go-between in the purchase, which was previously divided between several rather complicated ownerships.

Having acquired the site, Keiller was anxious to know more about it, and with Crawford's assistance, he organized a first campaign of archaeological excavation on the site. However, all was even now not straightforward since the archaeology of Wiltshire was regarded as a private preserve by the curator of the museum at Devizes, Maud Cunnington, and the members of the Wiltshire Archaeological Society. They did not look favourably upon an unknown individual investigating the site, even though he was now its owner, and doubted his archaeological credentials. Crawford arranged a compromise, and it was agreed that the elderly Harold St George Gray, who had excavated Avebury between 1909 and 1922 (see p. 123–6), would oversee the excavation, and be the nominal director.

Gray had been trained by the great archaeologist, General Pitt-Rivers, from about 1875, and in many ways, although competent, he was still

1 Windmill Hill from the square enclosure with a burial ceremony under way (Judith Dobie)

2

3

2 The facade of the West Kennet long barrow (Caroline Malone)

3 West Kennet long barrow, showing a burial taking place just before the final closure of the tomb (Judith Dobie)

4 The Sanctuary as it might have appeared during its final phase (Judith Dobie)

5 Silbury Hill from the air (Mick Aston)

6 The summit of Silbury under excavation in 1969-70, showing the chalk walls (Alexander Keiller Museum, Avebury)

7 Silbury under construction with hoards of people working on the transportation
of chalk and soil (Judith Dobie)

8

9

8 Avebury from the air: the south-west sector (English Heritage)

9 General view of Avebury from the air (Mick Aston)

10 Avebury henge under construction, showing the ditches being excavated and the stones dragged into position (Judith Dobie)

11   **11** A harvest ceremony taking place at the c̊ave in the northern circle of Avebury
(Judith Dobie)

46 *Excavations on Windmill Hill in 1925. Harold St George Gray in the deck chair inspecting a find passed to him by Alexander Keiller. Note the photographic and survey equipment in the background.*

inclined to use the techniques of the nineteenth century. This soon proved to be his weakness in his relations with Keiller. Keiller was an innovator, and delighted in the latest techniques and equipment. The first archaeological season in the summer of 1925 was a testing time for both men. Gray insisted on traditional trenches; Keiller insisted on immaculate survey and precise recording methods including photographs of everything. Keiller kept everything that was excavated; Gray, on the other hand, saw no use for animal bone and had it reburied in the ditches; and from the diaries that both men kept, there appears to have been considerable tension and disagreement. However, Gray could not be removed until it was universally agreed that Keiller knew how to excavate properly (**46**).

A longer second season in 1926 followed, and Keiller began to gather around him a loyal and skilled team of excavators, both archaeologists and local labourers. By 1927, Keiller was able to take over exclusive direction of the site. Gray's old trenches were re-excavated so that items which had been discarded could be recovered, and from then on, the project insisted on scientific precision and dedicated hard work. Keiller employed secretaries to type the catalogues, female archaeologists to sort the flint and pot, as well as the team of diggers and workmen (**47**). The project continued each summer until 1929, with all the finds being taken off to Keiller's private museum in his house in London. Before long, the restored pots became famous, since they were then unique examples, and the quality of Keiller's work was widely acknowledged. Towards the end of the project, late one night in the Red Lion Hotel in Avebury where the team was staying, Keiller suddenly announced that he intended to buy Avebury, its circle, its manor and the site of the Avenue, and to undertake excavation of the site recorded long before by William Stukeley. In this way

47 *The Windmill Hill excavation team in 1927, with Keiller seated at centre.*

Keiller's involvement with Avebury and its Neolithic archaeology was to continue.

Initially, Keiller bought Avebury with the primary intention of preservation and intended to excavate only parts of it, so that the site could be understood. He still lived in London, and took all the excavated finds back to his own private museum, where any interested scholars could study them. However, as time went on, he became determined that Avebury should become a publically-owned ancient monument.

Once his excavations were complete, he began to negotiate with the National Trust, hoping that the site would pass into their ownership for perpetuity. Once Keiller had bought Avebury Manor in 1934, he moved his private museum to the coach house, calling it the Morven Institute of Archaeological Research, and opening it regularly to the public with displays of archaeological material including finds from Windmill Hill. Thus the archaeological collection which forms an important part of Avebury Museum today had its beginnings in Keiller's excavations on Windmill Hill.

5

The long barrows

The burial places of the Neolithic farmers of the Avebury area offer a direct and tangible link with the first farming communities, since one can still enter the tomb at West Kennet and experience something of the mystery that must have pervaded the site in the Neolithic period. Although the attention of most visitors of Avebury is drawn only to the famous West Kennet long barrow, there are in fact the remains of at least another 27 similar structures in the Avebury area (**48**). Such a concentration of long barrows within a restricted area is almost unique in southern Britain, and their forms and structures are also unusual. They are a further indication of the importance of the area in Neolithic times.

48 *Map of long barrows in the Avebury area.*

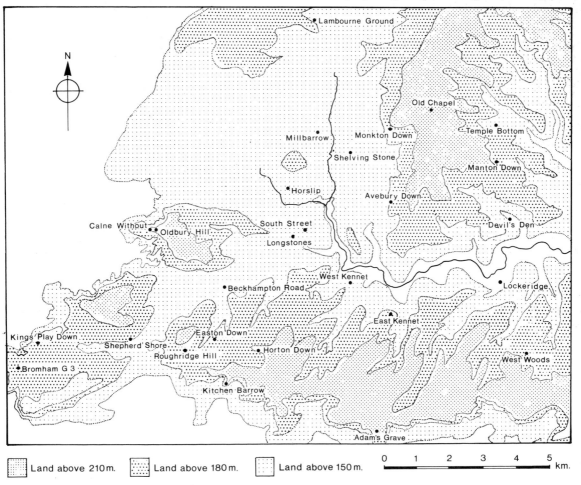

Land above 210 m. Land above 180 m. Land above 150 m.

0 1 2 3 4 5 km.

The Avebury barrows form a dense group on the northern chalkland of Wiltshire. There is a clear distinction between the Avebury barrows and other groups in the Stonehenge area, the Dorset Ridgeway and the Cotswolds. The actual forms of the Avebury barrows fall into three main types, and in some instances these different structural elements are found incorporated together, under the earth and rubble mounds which cover the tombs. The most durable and impressive type of barrow is the type with stone chambers: these have large megalithic stone slabs forming a passage, and radiating chambers for the burials. The West and East Kennet barrows are the best preserved examples of this type. A different, but possibly related form, is a type with timber chambers, where wooden posts, planks and stakes were used to form simple compartments within the earthen mound. Yet another type appear to have been formed without any chambers at all: these were simply piles of earth, flint, sarsen and chalk rubble, sometimes incorporating simple cists of small stones. The West Kennet barrow

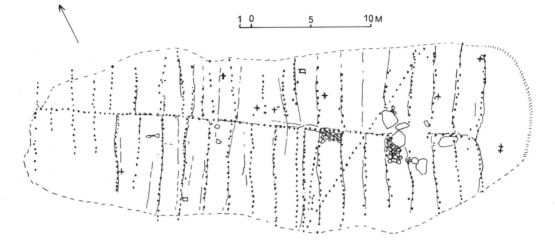

49 *(Above) Plan of the hurdle partitions found in South Street long barrow (crosses = antlers; squares = ox scapulae).*

50 *Plan of hurdle partitions found beneath Beckhampton Road long barrow (black triangles = ox skulls).*

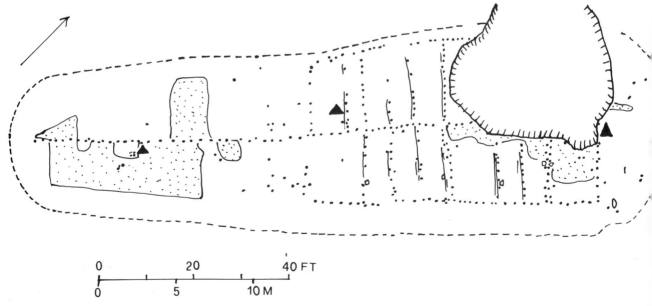

incorporates two styles, with a megalithic chambered east end, and what appears to be an unchambered earth and rubble barrow at the west end. South Street barrow was an unchambered type, with flimsy rows of hurdles dividing the interior into neat cells (**49**). The Beckhampton Road barrow was similarly constructed with stakes and chalk rubble (**50**).

The Avebury barrows incorporate elements of several distinctive regional distributions. Megalithic portal and chamber tombs are typical of Wales and the south-west of Britain, whereas the earthen long barrow is typical of the Wessex chalklands. Both these general types, together with other specific regional styles, are found at Avebury. Elsewhere, the most usual tomb types in northern Britain were the passage graves and in the east, square or rectangular mortuary enclosures and timber-chambered earthen mounds such as Haddenham in the Cambridgeshire Fens.

Although it is unlikely that long barrows, or indeed any particularly formal burial monuments, were constructed from the moment that farming was adopted in Britain, long barrows and their megalithic counterparts in the western zone of the country, date from the second phase of tomb building in Britain. The earliest tombs were constructed from about 3600–2800 BC and varied regionally. The earliest enclosures and cairns were frequently added to and modified in the centuries after their construction and some excavated examples are known from central southern England, including Wayland's Smithy and Ascott-under-Wychwood (Oxfordshire). In these examples, an earlier cairn-type structure was added to with larger and more formal stone or wooden chambers. In general, the later and modified tombs survive best, and date from the period c.3000–2200 BC.

The following table gives a rough guide to the phasing of the Avebury tombs and similar tombs nearby, outside the Avebury area:

C14 date	approx. BC dates	stone chambers	wood chambers	unchambered
3415 + 180 bc	4350		Lambourne, Berkshire	
3240 + 150 bc				Windmill Hill, Horslip
3230 + 180 bc			Fussell's Lodge, Wilts	
3248 + 225 bc				
3070 + 92 bc				
2992 + 74 bc				
2943 + 70 bc		Ascott-under-Wychwood		
2785 + 70 bc				
2764 + 166 bc				
2495 + 61 bc				
2820 + 130 bc		Wayland's Smithy, Berkshire		
2875 + 90 bc		West Kennet barrow		
2830 + 90 bc		West Kennet barrow		
2750 + 80 bc	3500	West Kennet barrow		
?		East Kennet barrow		
?		Millbarrow, Winterbourne Monkton		
?		Manton Down barrow		
2721 + 150 bc				Nutbane barrow, Dorset (old soil surface)
2810 + 130 bc				
2710 + 130 bc				South Street, Avebury
2750 + 135 bc				
2670 + 140 bc				
2580 + 110 bc				
2560 + 103 bc				Normanton Down, Amesbury,
2517 + 90 bc	3000			Beckhampton Rd., Avebury

Distribution of long barrows in the Avebury area

The construction of large and impressive tombs was an activity intended more to impress the living community than was necessary to honour the dead individuals placed within them. There are many theories that attempt to explain why such massive and labour intensive tombs should have been built. In the Avebury area, which stretches from Knap Hill in the south, north to Winterbourne Bassett, east to Lockeridge and west beyond Calne, the number of tombs known from the 1500–2000 years of the Neolithic, although great by most Neolithic distributions, would never have been sufficient to serve the burial needs of all the communities in the area. Not all the tombs that survive are as massive as West Kennet, and many less impressive constructions may well have disappeared. However, the surviving examples should be ample data to provide a picture of the construction and use of the tombs of the Neolithic.

The large Megalithic barrows such as the East and West Kennet barrows are generally located on the summit of hills around Avebury, where they stand out prominently, and can be seen from many directions. The later and unchambered barrows such as South Street and Beckhampton are not prominent, being located on land which is comparatively level. The fact that no human remains whatsoever have been found in either of these later barrows is surprising, and it has been suggested that they might have acted as mausolea or cenotaphs, memorials to the dead. Curiously, both barrows contained deposits of animal bones in the staked-out chambers, South Street barrow having a number of ox skulls, and Beckhampton Road having deer antler and other animal bones (49). Another suggestion, that probes more closely into the function of the barrows, may be more plausible. The barrows may have functioned as territorial markers, acting as visible claims to land that long-dead ancestors had staked out. As the environment of Avebury became more densely populated over the centuries, and more and more groups of people inhabited the former territories of old lineage groups, the new groups also required an 'ancestral tomb', so that they too, belonged to the territory. Thus a convincingly old-looking mound might have been a sufficient symbol for new groups to qualify as members of the community with their own bogus 'ancestral' barrow. In effect, such a barrow would be making similar claims to antiquity as would 'Stockbroker's Tudor' architecture in an otherwise traditional village! The importance of the barrows as the major monuments in the earlier and middle Neolithic period declined by the time the other major Avebury monuments were being constructed, and from being principal ceremonial constructions, assumed a secondary importance.

The Manton Down barrow

The Kennett valley appears to have been an important focus for barrows, and a number have been recorded from the valley and its small tributaries. Of considerable importance was the presence of the sarsen stones, which were, and still are, plentiful on the hillslopes and valleys flanking the Marlborough Downs. The Manton Down barrow survived until 1952 as a megalithic structure with chambers and earth mound. In that year a bulldozer removed the earth barrow, to reveal a sarsen cairn. The site was then excavated and Windmill Hill pottery together with an ox skull was found. There had been a forecourt on the south-east end which had been blocked by small sarsen slabs, and ditches either side of the mound which had a length of only 66 ft (20 m).

The East Kennet barrow

Of the two best known barrows, at West and East Kennet, the latter has never been investigated. It is in fact longer than West Kennet, being 345 ft (105 m) long, as against 330 ft (100 m), and 100 ft (30 m) wide as against 82 ft (25 m); it stands to a height of 14 ft (4.2 m), in comparison to the 10 ft (3 m) of the West Kennet. It is oriented south-east to north-west, and West Kennet is oriented east to west. In construction, the mound appears to be made up of a massive core of sarsen stones. However, the site has never been subjected to any largescale excavation, and it may be the last remaining long barrow of any consequence in Wiltshire to have survived the ravages of enthusiastic archaeologists. Despite this, large trees have been allowed to grow over it, probably damaging the interior chambers and their contents. The barrow now appears to stand isolated from the rest of the Avebury complex, but it is very much part of it, being within easy sight of the Sanctuary and West Kennet long barrow. On one faint aerial photograph taken some forty years ago

51 *Aerial view of the East Kennet long barrow covered in trees, looking east.*

a possible cursus was noticed running from the north-east to the south-west, past the north-west end of the barrow. If this line is indeed a cursus, it is the only one in north Wessex, and would add to the significance of the ritual landscape of Avebury.

Adam's Grave

Some 1.9 miles (3 km) to the south stands Adam's Grave, on the summit of the chalk escarpment overlooking the vale of Pewsey, adjacent to the causewayed enclosure of Knap Hill. Adam's grave is probably the most impressive of all the Avebury barrows, since its location is so spectacular, and the tomb itself is comparatively well-preserved. The mound is made to appear all the more impressive by its cunning use of the hillslope and the deep lateral ditches at either side. The antiquary Colt Hoare recorded it in his *Ancient History of Wiltshire* (1821), describing its ridge as 'more acute than any I have seen'. The barrow is 213 ft (65 m) in length, and varies in width from 92 ft (28 m) at its south-eastern end, to 53 ft (16 m) at its north-western end. The interior of the mound is made up of sarsen blocks, probably forming chambers similar to West Kennet. Much of the tomb may remain intact, (particularly the façade area), but excavations by Thurnam in the 1860s, and others before him, left it disturbed and partially

destroyed. Skeletal remains of several individuals and a leaf-shaped arrowhead were recovered, but now only the arrowhead survives, in the vaults of the British Museum.

The West Kennet barrow

The barrow belonging to the Avebury group which has been most comprehensively studied is the West Kennet long barrow, and it can still be seen in its restored splendour (**colour plates 2,3**). Its first builders began with less grandiose ideas than the great edifice which eventually appeared. The barrow was begun very early in the history of Avebury, perhaps even before the first activities on Windmill Hill, *c.*3500–3700 BC. It was first marked out on the ground, directly onto the green turf of the hillside. It was lined up east to west, and had its main opening on the east end. The central line of the barrow was first defined by a mound of rough sarsen stones and boulders, picked up from the immediate area and heaped into a well-defined ridge about 6 ft (2 m) high. Within this mound, there may have been roughly defined stone chambers, since the excavations in 1955–6 revealed lines of stones that might have been intended as structural elements such as burial cists in the early barrow. The great stone chambers at the east end were probably not added until a later stage. The second phase of building was of chalk rubble, heaped over the original sarsen core, using the chalk quarried directly from the two lateral ditches at either side of the barrow. These two ditches were probably dug rather haphazardly by small gangs of workers, since they formed a very rough and irregular shape along the sides and base. The ditches reached a depth of 4–6 ft (1.5–2 m) and were about 23 ft (7 m) wide. On the mounds, hard chalk from the lowest part of the ditch covered a layer of mixed chalk and soil and when first dug would have made a striking white ridge of chalk on the hillside. Only after several years would soil have begun to cover the barrow, merging the monument back into the green landscape around it. The ditches running along the length of the barrow filled up quite rapidly with the loose soil and chalk falling from the mound. Their secondary filling appears to have occurred during the later Neolithic period, since sherds of Peterborough pottery were found in the upper fill of the ditch.

The great megalithic chambers at the east end may have been part of the original plan for

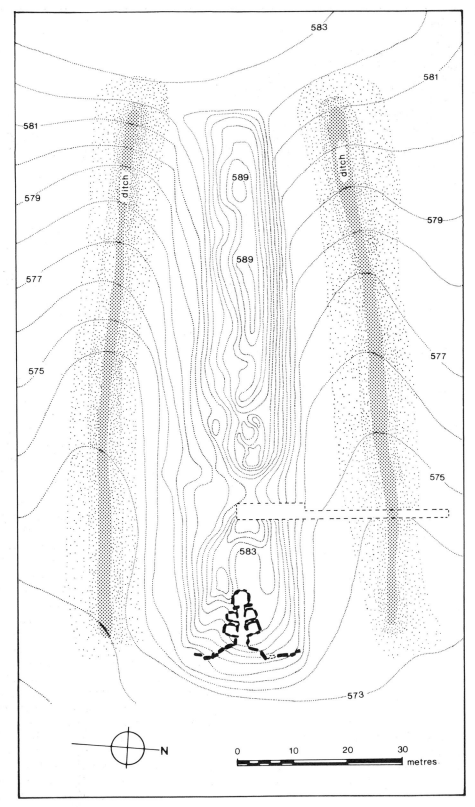

583

581

581

579

589

577

589

579

575

577

575

583

573

N

0   10   20   30
metres

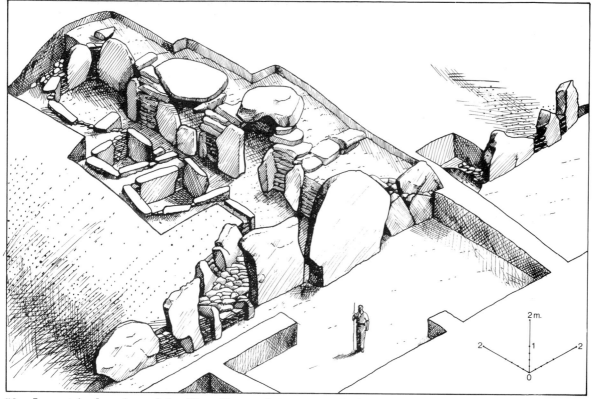

53 *Isometric drawing of the West Kennet long barrow, showing the stone chambers, the passage and the blocking stones in the crescent-shaped forecourt (after Piggott 1963).*

the barrow, or, as at a number of other sites such as Wayland's Smithy, they may have been added when the barrow became more important, and burial ritual changed. The rites might have required open chambers rather than small cist-like burials in the rubble or a wooden mortuary house, and this may have been a reason for the construction of the megalithic east end of the barrow. Excavation has still not explored the bulk of the earthen long barrow at the west end, so it is impossible to know either the sequence of construction, or what is contained within its length.

The stone chambers were built according to a definite plan, which was carefully measured

52 *Plan of the West Kennet long barrow, showing the lateral ditches, earthern mound and stone chambers at the east end. The excavation trench shown was dug in 1955–6 (after Piggott 1963).*

out before the great stones were put into position. The passage and the four side and single end chambers are classic examples of the Severn-Cotswold 'transepted gallery-grave', a type that may have evolved first in the coastal region of the Loire in west France, and which became popular in south-west Britain and the Channel Islands. This type of tomb always incorporated side chambers with a passage leading off from a forecourt, where burial rituals may have taken place. At West Kennet, the passage leads into the tomb from a crescent-shaped forecourt facing east, which was later blocked with the massive upright stones that fill the space today. The great sarsen stones were selected from surrounding valleys, and dragged up to the barrow, where they were set upright into shallow holes to form the walls of the chambers. The smaller gaps between the large stones were filled, curiously enough, by imported Corallian limestone from the Calne district 7 miles (11 km) to the west. Other 'foreign' stone was also brought in from the oolitic limestone outcrops further west. Why such care should have been taken over the selection of stone for the interior walling of the tomb is a mystery, but similar stone has

54 *The chambers and passage at the West Kennet long barrow.*

also been found in the other Avebury barrows at South Street, Shepherd's Shore, Easton Down, Kitchen Barrow, and Adam's Grave. Such stone was also found in the square enclosure on Windmill Hill and in the West Kennet Avenue occupation site, and may have been a special component in the ritual associated with burial in the Avebury area.

The passage of the barrow was capped by large sarsen stones resting on the uprights, but in the chambers a form of corbelling, where each stone course projected above the one below to form a vaulted, beehive-like roof, was employed. Traces of this can still be seen, although the chambers have suffered from collapse and early destructive excavations which entered the barrow through the roofs. Over the large west chamber, a huge capstone was supported on corbels, although this has now been replaced by a concrete slab.

Several of the sarsen stones selected for the walls had been lying in the open countryside, and had already been employed for other uses, principally for the grinding and sharpening of stone axes, before the Neolithic builders chose them for the tomb. Stone 18 in the passage shows areas where grinding took place, and stone 43 in the blocking of the forecourt has areas of axe sharpening. It is quite likely that these stones were once located conveniently close to areas of settlement or activity. On the Ridgeway, not far from where Green Street joins the path, there is a similar stone, showing areas of grinding as well as grooves where the edges were sharpened, and the stones from the barrow were once almost certainly similarly located.

The interior of the completed tomb would have been dark and watertight. Access was probably restricted by some sort of barricade at the entrance, and within, the corpse of the

55 *The stone chambers of the West Kennet long barrow with their contents (after Piggott 1963).*

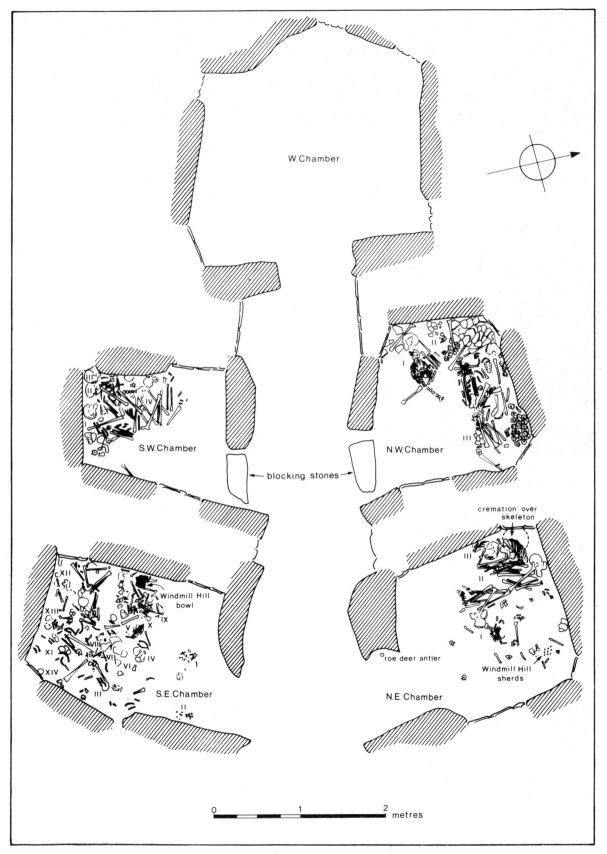

W.Chamber

S.W.Chamber

N.W.Chamber

→ blocking stones ←

cremation over
skeleton

roe deer antler

Windmill Hill
bowl

S.E.Chamber

Windmill Hill
sherds

N.E.Chamber

0   1   2 metres

dead disintegrated slowly and noisomely. Few would have wished to enter the tomb until the bones were finally clean, and those allowed to enter may have held some special role within Avebury society. The bones of previous burials were tidied into heaps before the next person was interred in the space within. The contents of the chambers when excavated included the bones of at least 46 inviduals, although for the most part, each person was represented only by a few, often scattered, fragments of bone (**55**). Many of the individuals buried were children or infants, and it is interesting that young children had sufficient status in the society of Avebury to qualify for burial in the tomb. In many societies (ancient and modern) children below a certain age or prior to their formal initiation into adult society, are not considered to have sufficient status for inclusion in collective burials.

di

At West Kennet the internal organization of the tomb appears to have been quite important, and different chambers were generally used for different age groups. The large chamber at the west end had a preponderance of male adult burials, whereas the south-west and north-west chambers had both male and female adults. The south-east chamber on the other hand, was reserved mainly for children and juveniles, and at the opposite extreme, the north-east chamber contained old people. The selection of the chambers may have been regarded as symbolic, with a clear geometrical arrangement of opposing or complementary age and sex groups.

The primary burials were laid directly onto the original turf floor of the tomb. Soon others were inserted, and some of the first burials were moved to the back of the chambers, often with bones such as the skulls and long bones being removed for ceremonies elsewhere, such as on the causewayed enclosures and within the Avebury henge. In some cases, the new burials were placed almost directly above earlier burials, or bones were collected up, and stacked against the walls, as in the north-west and south-west chambers. As well as the skeletal remains, cremated bodies were also deposited, and included at least two individuals, a male and a female. This was a departure from the norm, and some of the other bones also showed signs of scorching, perhaps as a result of close proximity to fires lit when the funerary feasts or sacrifices took place outside the barrow, before the final disposal of the bodies. Animal bones

found in the tomb probably also derived from these ritual feasts and sacrifices, and became confused with the human bones in the tomb.

The tomb went on being used for generations, and indeed, may have been in use for a thousand years or more. The final burials to be placed in the tomb were during the Beaker period, perhaps c.2200 BC. The final burial was of an elderly man in the north-east chamber, who was placed on a specially-laid floor of pavings in the north-east chamber. He had a leaf-shaped arrowhead in his throat, and this was probably the cause of his death. Soon after this, the tomb, which had become thoroughly dilapidated, was filled quite intentionally with quantities of earth, rubble, chalk, sarsen and domestic rubbish. It had clearly been brought in from different sources, and laid down in layers, covering all the burials and collapsed walling of the tombs. Similar domestic refuse appears to have been dumped in the Sanctuary and in other contemporary barrows. Quite why is a matter for speculation, but perhaps the rubbish came from another ceremonial site, and was regarded as having special properties which enriched or protected the primary contents of the tomb.

Once the passage and chambers were filled, the blocking of the entrance took place, thus closing the tomb. Great sarsens were selected and dragged into position, forming a line across the crescent-shaped former entrance. Few, if any, of the other barrows in the area seem to have been treated in the same way.

Contents of the chambers of the West Kennet long barrow

West chamber: 5 adult males; ? 1 child

South west chamber: 1 child; 1 young female with abnormal skull; 1 old female; 1 part of a 16 to 20-year-old youth; 2 infants; fragments of 3 males and 2 females; 5 mandibles

South-east chamber: 1 male; 1 female; 5 children aged 3 to 7; 5 infants; 1 foetus

North-west chamber: 1 old female; 1 old male; 1 semi-articulated young male; bones of at least 2 males and 4 females; mandibles of 3 females; pile of vertebrae and long bones

North-east chamber: 1 young female; 1 old male with arrowhead; 1 old female; cremated remains of male and female; roe deer antler at entrance

(West chamber dug by Thurnam 1859, other chambers dug by Piggott and Atkinson 1955–6.)

76

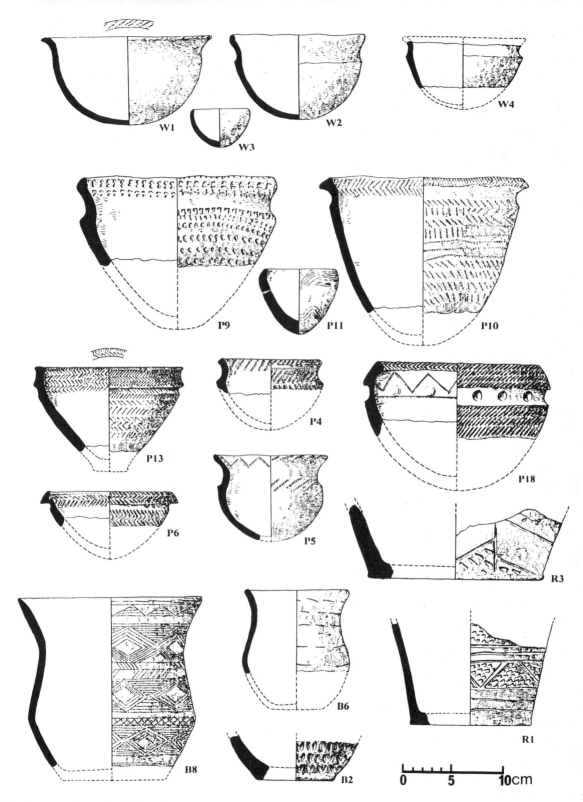

56 *Pottery from the West Kennet long barrow:*
W = Earlier-Neolithic Windmill Hill wares
P = Peterborough Middle Neolithic wares;
R = Later Neolithic Rinyo-Clacton-Grooved
wares; B = Beaker wares (after Piggott 1963).

The people buried in West Kennet were accompanied by grave goods which may have symbolized their position in Avebury society. Over 250 pots of many styles were deposited in the tomb, but when they were excavated they

were in fragments, like the bodies they were with, and scattered amongst the debris of the filling and reorganization that had been a feature of the rituals of burial. Although the early Windmill Hill style of pottery was found in the lowest levels of turf in the tomb, the pottery that was more usually left as grave gifts for the dead was of the later period and included Peterborough types (Mortlake, Fengate and Ebbsfleet styles) of the period 3000–2500 BC. Later still, wares of the Beaker period from c.2500–2000 BC typified by the decorated Beakers and the associated Rinyo-Clacton style of late Neolithic pottery became

57 Flint tools from the West Kennet long barrow: 1–2 = leaf-shaped arrowheads; 3 = Petit-tranchet arrowhead; 4–7 = serrated flakes; 8 = broken chisel; 9–12 = horseshoe-shaped scrapers; 13 = end scraper; 14, 17 edge scrapers; 15 = double-ended scraper; 16 = straight end scraper; 18 = side scraper; 19-25 = scrapers; polished knife (after Piggott 1963).

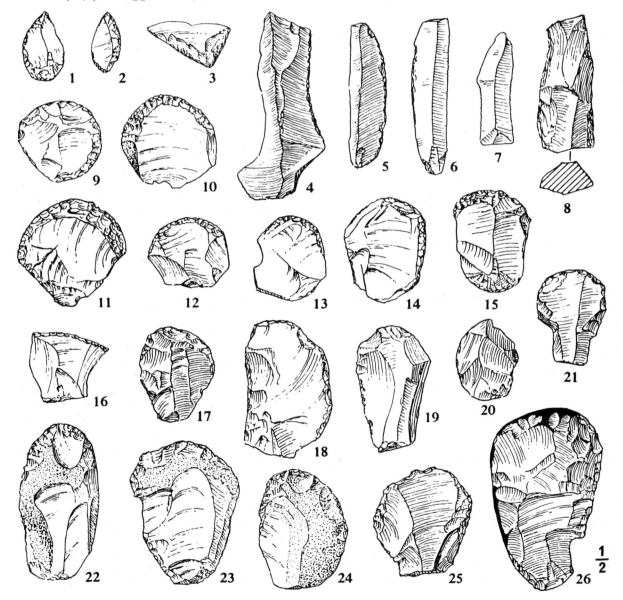

more prevalent (**56**). Much of the pottery had presumably arrived as complete vessels, to be stored in a temporary repository outside the tomb, and was broken whilst being dumped together with all the domestic material and rubbish in the tomb.

Significantly, the most nearly complete vessel was the beaker (**56 B**) that accompanied the final burial of the old man in the north-east chamber. Soon after his interment, as already stated, the tomb was closed and filled with the domestic material which included many broken sherds of pottery, and no further tidying-up of the bodies or their grave goods took place. The careful placement of some of the pottery sherds may also have been symbolic: small fragments were pushed into the cracks and crevices of the tomb, and into the skulls and between the bones of some of the remaining skeletons.

Other items were placed in the tomb including a number of flint tools, such as scrapers and knives, and bone tools including points and toggles, perhaps from clothing (**57**). There were also shale, bone and shell beads, probably from necklaces and jewellery. There were a number of fragments of animal bone, including a deer antler placed at the entrance to one of the chambers. The animal bones may have arrived in the form of complete joints of meat, at the time when the bodies were committed for burial, ready for ritual feasts. These animal remains may also have been carefully placed in the tomb, with the north-east chamber having a predominance of cattle bone and the greatest number of grave goods, and the north-west, south-west and south-east chambers mainly having sheep and pig bones.

Examination of the skeletal remains found in the 1955–6 excavations revealed that the population buried in the West Kennet long barrow had numerous medical problems, some of which probably proved fatal. The infants and children could have died from a variety of typical juvenile diseases, including measles, pneumonia and influenza, which leave no scar on the osteological remains. The adults, on the other hand, showed osteological signs of many medical conditions. Damp, cold living conditions meant that nearly all the adults over thirty years of age suffered from spinal arthritis; two also had badly affected hip joints; and others had deformed arms, wrists, hands and feet. Males suffered from bone fractures to a far greater extent than the females, suggesting

that either their work in agriculture and animal husbandry was more strenuous than that of the females, or that they indulged in physical combat with their rivals and enemies. Three of the most complete male skeletons had healed fractures in their arms, and one had an abscess in the head of the humerus which had clearly affected the surrounding muscle. The same man also had a fractured arm, which was still healing at the time of his death.

Examination of the teeth of the skeletons revealed absceses and impacted wisdom teeth, while several of the older individuals had very worn teeth. Of the twenty-one jaws found, five had peridontal disease of the jaw. Two jaws were found with no teeth left at all. However, in other respects the Neolithic population apparently had healthy teeth, with few cavities or signs of decay.

The presence of congenital diseases can indicate that skeletal remains belonged to individuals who might have been related. In the case of West Kennet, spina bifida was found in a surprising number of bodies, suggesting that they may have come from a single family group. Spondylochisis of the spine was identified in a further three individuals and this may indicate a linkage with the spina bifida cases. Several of the diseases identified within the skeletons might have caused death; but in one or two cases it was clear that death was from recent injury, as in the case of the male with an arrowhead in his neck.

Excavation and subsequent history of the barrow
The West Kennet barrow has a long recorded history, like the other Avebury sites. It was first described by John Aubrey who sketched it and several others for his *Monumenta Britannica* some time during the period 1665–93. Curiously, he showed the barrow with small sarsen stones running along either side of the mound. He described it thus: 'on the brow of the hill, south from West Kynnet, is this monument, but without any name... but at the end, only rude greyweather-stones tumbled together; the barrow is about half a yard high'. Aubrey was again directed to the tomb by Dr Toope of Marlborough, who wrote to him about his other discoveries at the Sanctuary in 1685. The doctor had found workmen digging up bones at the Sanctuary, and he '... quickly perceiv'd that they were humane, and came the next day and

The Long Barrow S. of Silbury Hill.

An Archdruids barrow.

58 *Stukeley's sketch of the West Kennet long barrow, which he called the 'Archdruid's barrow'.*

dugg for them, and stored myselfe with many bushells, of which I made a noble medicine that relieved my distressed neighbours'. The considerable disturbance noted by Stukeley at West Kennet several decades later was probably caused by Dr Toope, who, as Aubrey also recorded, 'was lately at the Golgotha again to supply a defect of medicine he had from hence'.

William Stukeley took a great interest in the 'Archdruids Barrow' as he called it, and also sketched it for his book *Abury* published in 1743 (**58**). At that time the barrow was crossed by a track but was otherwise fairly intact, in spite of Dr Toope's diggings, although Stukeley wrote that 'Dr Took, as they call him, has miserably defaced South Long Barrow by digging half the length of it. It was most neatly smoothed to a sharp ridge'. He also described the barrow: 'It stands east and west, pointing to the Dragon's head on Overton Hill. A very operose congeries of huge stones upon the east end, and upon part of its back or ridge; pil'd one upon the other, with no little labour; doubtless in order to form a sufficient chamber for the remains of the person there buried: not easily to be disturbed. The whole tumulus is an

excessively large mound of earth, 180 cubits long, ridg'd up like a house.'

The barrow survived in spite of being mutilated by a farm track crossing the mound; being stripped of its turf by local tenants; and dug into for chalk and flint; and does not appear to have attracted much attention until the middle of the following century when a Dr Thurnam excavated the passage and west chamber in 1859, in a search for early examples of human remains. Dr Thurnham was the Medical Superintendent of the Wiltshire County Asylum at Devizes and an amateur archaeologist, who was fascinated by prehistoric skulls and bones. His excavation explored part of the east end of the barrow. Permission had not been given for any of the surface stone to be removed, so Thurnam had to tunnel under and around the remaining capstones. Whilst the work was under way, one capstone, weighing 3 tons, fell into the west chamber and had to be removed by the workmen. Eventually the whole west chamber was cleared, and the skeletal remains removed. Then about 15 ft (4.6 m) of the passage was also excavated, until a blockage of large stones made progress impossible. Thurnam decided at this point that the barrow had no further chambers, and that he had excavated all he needed to. This was fortunate, since he missed the four side chambers and the rest of the passage. In

59 *Aerial view of the West Kennet long barrow after excavation and restoration.*

spite of the rather unscientific method he used to excavate, Thurnam nevertheless recorded useful details about the interior fill of the barrow, remarking upon the chalk rubble, the sooty soil and the thickness of the different layers. He also kept all the skeletal remains, together with his other collections of 'Ancient British' material, and they are now in the Duckworth collection at Cambridge University.

The only scientific excavations on the barrow took place in 1955–6, when Professors Piggott and Atkinson made a complete study of the chambered end of the barrow and sampled the ditch and long mound. This was done so that the barrow could be opened to visitors. The great closing slabs at the east end had mostly fallen flat on the ground, and much of the disturbed passage and the roofs to the chambers had fallen in (**23**). The slow and careful task of clearing the fallen debris and the upper layers of the secondary fill then took place, before it was found that Thurnam had failed to discover the four side chambers of the barrow. This was an unexpected bonus for the excavators, who had expected that the bulk of the contents had been removed or destroyed in earlier excavations. The bones and skeletal remains were found almost intact, and the contents were carefully planned *in situ* and removed for further study.

Other sites have since been dug, building on the experience gained from the West Kennet excavations, but nevertheless, West Kennet remains one of the classic excavations of its type. The site was restored after the excavations, using all the original sarsen stones, which were replaced in their original holes, or, in the case of the capstones, on their original orthostats. The great capstone over the west chamber had long since disappeared, and was replaced by a concrete slab with glass insets, so that light could penetrate into the chamber. The original Corallian limestone from Calne had largely disintegrated and was replaced by stone quarried from the same area, in an attempt to make the reconstruction as authentic as possible.

6

The Sanctuary and the avenues

The Sanctuary

The Sanctuary on Overton Hill was thus named by the first antiquary who recorded the site, John Aubrey, in 1648. He rather surprisingly claimed that this was the name given it by the local people. The name stuck, and succeeding antiquaries and archaeologists have continued to use it. Overton Hill stands to the south-east of Avebury, and is crossed by the modern A4

60 *Aerial view looking north up the Ridgeway, showing the Sanctuary on the west side, Bronze Age barrows on the east and the Roman road and prehistoric field systems beyond. The dark stain in the crop north of the Sanctuary is the site of a now destroyed stone circle.*

road, beside the ancient Ridgeway path. It is prominent and highly visible from all directions, and this is probably the reason why it was chosen 5000 years ago as the location for a cult centre.

The Sanctuary itself seems to have consisted of roofed, circular buildings, one replacing another on the same site over a period of several hundred years. Initially the buildings were built of wood, but in the final phase, sarsen stones were incorporated, and the whole site was linked to Avebury by the West Kennet Avenue of standing stones. Large circular buildings of the 'Sanctuary' type are known from other sites in Wessex, and are in all cases associated with henge monuments. Woodhenge, east of Stonehenge, was the first to be discovered, but there the circular building was surrounded by a small 'henge-like' ditch and bank. The great henge of Durrington Walls beside Woodhenge has more than one circular building, one near its south entrance being of complex design, much like the Sanctuary, and a smaller one lying to the north. Midway between Avebury and Stonehenge is the Marden henge in the Vale of Pewsey, which also contains a comparable circular building, and in Dorset the henge at Mount Pleasant contained at least two circular buildings (**61**). Thus large Wessex henges characteristically appear to contain circular buildings. Indeed, at Avebury itself the two inner circles, which are both in stone, may have had earlier wooden predecessors before the final stone ones were erected. Stonehenge, only a small henge in comparison, contains the

61 *Wessex henges and their various arrangements of circular buildings and circles.*

Durrington Walls

Avebury

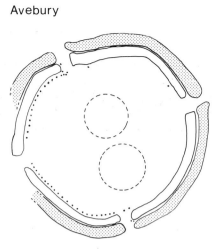

0   100   200   300   400
Metres

Mount Pleasant

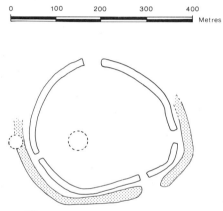

Marden

Woodhenge

0   50
Metres

Bank

N

elaborate building of upright sarsen stones and the imported bluestones making up the impressive stone circle. The function of these structures has been the focus of much speculation, and Stonehenge in particular has been provisionally identified as an observatory and as a form of calendar. The Sanctuary, on the other hand, has usually been considered to be a mortuary house.

The evolution of the Sanctuary

The Sanctuary was first constructed about 3000 BC and its site may have been a new clearing on Overton Hill, or may have been already regarded as of ceremonial or ritual importance. The first structure was a small and simply constructed round hut, measuring 15 ft (4.5 m) in diameter. There were eight posts supporting

62 *The phases of building at the Sanctuary, and possible reconstructions.*

the outer wall and a single central post to support what was probably a conical thatched roof. Pottery of Windmill Hill type and Ebbsfleet ware was found in the post holes and appears to represent the earliest material on the site. This first hut, perhaps that of a holy man, may have been the *raison d'être* for the Sanctuary site later becoming such an important location.

The second phase of the Sanctuary, perhaps 100 to 200 years later, saw a new extended building on the same site, which completely enclosed the first hut, which was probably still standing, within a much larger and more massive structure. There were two rings of post holes, very much larger in size than the first

63 *(Right) Plan of the Sanctuary and its excavations in 1930, showing the four building phases and the Avenue.*

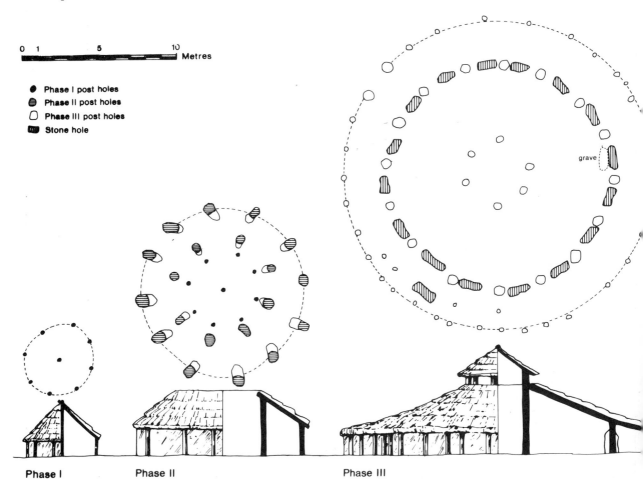

0   1   5   10
                                        Metres

● Phase I post holes
⊜ Phase II post holes
◯ Phase III post holes
▨ Stone hole

grave

Phase I   Phase II   Phase III

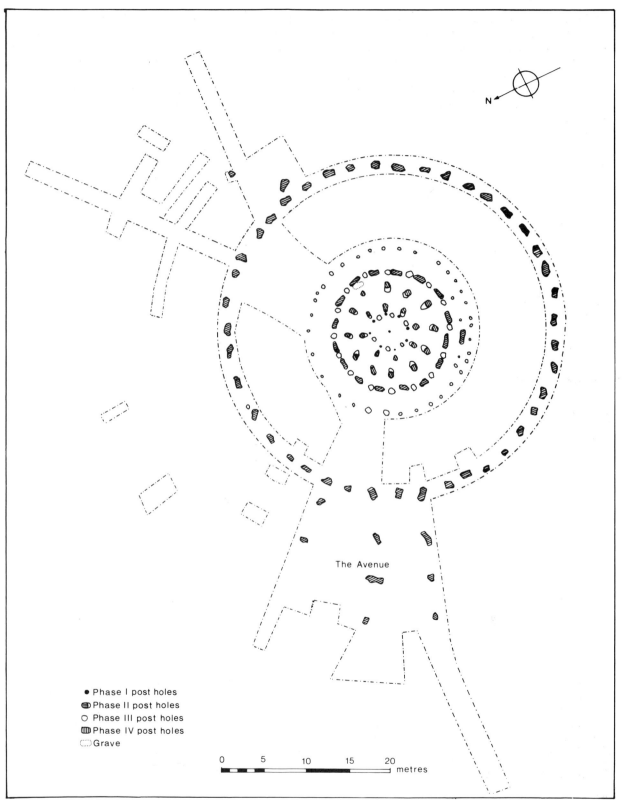

N

● Phase I post holes
⬮ Phase II post holes
○ Phase III post holes
◍ Phase IV post holes
⬭ Grave

The Avenue

0   5   10   15   20
                    metres

hut, with a diameter of 37 ft (11.2 m). The new posts of this building were reset at some stage, since several of the post holes appear to show re-cutting.

The third phase appears to belong to the later Neolithic period, since Beaker pottery and Mortlake and Grooved ware types were found in association with the post holes of the third building on the site. This was almost twice as large as its predecessor, and had a diameter of 66 ft (20.1 m), and three concentric rings of post holes. Tentative reconstructions have suggested that the inner ring may have supported a central 'lantern' raised above the rest of the conical thatched roof (62). At some stage, possibly whilst the building was still standing, a sarsen stone circle was incorporated as part of the middle ring of posts, making a near-continuous internal wall of stones and posts. These stones may even have been an original part of the building of this phase. An entrance marked by two particularly massive posts was located on the north-west side of the hut, looking roughly towards Avebury. At the foot of one sarsen stone on the east side of the hut, a crouched Beaker burial of a youth was found, perhaps a dedicatory offering on the completion of this phase of the building.

The fourth phase appears to be contemporary with the West Kennet Avenue and possibly with the stone circles at Avebury. It consisted of a sarsen stone circle of 42 stones erected to form an outer boundary to the Sanctuary complex. This circle was 138 ft (40.2 m) in diameter, and was connected to the West Kennet Avenue by two stones set radially on its circumference more or less in line with the door posts of the third phase building (63). Another set of stones appears to have extended in the direction of Silbury Hill.

There are always problems in the reconstruction of the size and elevation of ancient buildings, when all the evidence we have is preserved in the ground plan of the structural posts and the relative depths of their setting in the ground. We can assume that the walls of the various phases of the Sanctuary were wattle and daub, since these materials were easily obtainable and commonly used in the Neolithic period. However, little evidence now remains even of these. Daub is occasionally preserved when it is burnt or at least 'cooked' *in situ*, occurring as lumps of hard clay material, showing the impressions of the wattles or twigs of

willow, hazel and other trees. The roofs of the Sanctuary buildings were almost certainly thatched with reeds or straw, and the slope of the roofs would necessarily have been very steep in order to ensure that rain drained off. The excavation of the Sanctuary took place in 1930, and although the site was comparatively well excavated for the time, no record was made of any floors or other internal features. Therefore we do not know whether the site had a beaten earth floor or was paved or plastered in some way.

The function of the Sanctuary remains a mystery, although a number of clues suggest possible uses of the site. The choice of site may have been made because it had traditional importance. The original building could have been the home of a 'wise man'. But whatever the original significance of the site was, it seems to have become a centre of some type of mortuary practice. Great numbers of human bones were found and recorded by earlier antiquaries, and more fragments were found in the 1930 excavations, scattered in the soil, together with rich evidence of feasts, suggesting that the rituals that took place in the round houses of the successive buildings on the Sanctuary site were accompanied by elaborate feasts involving

64 *Aerial view of the Sanctuary looking east. The line of the Avenue runs down the bottom of the picture following the right-hand side of the A4 road.*

animals and a great range of ceramic vessels. Circular buildings within other henges have produced comparable remains. There are many ethnographic examples of mortuary houses amongst tribal communities in undeveloped parts of the world. The corpse of a deceased person is laid out, perhaps on a platform, and left until either the flesh has rotted from the bones, or scavenging birds and animals have eaten it away. Once the bones are clean, they are collected up, and either placed in a tomb or scattered in some special place.

In the context of Neolithic Avebury, it seems quite likely that during its first phases the Sanctuary was connected to the rather grisly rites on Windmill Hill and in the long barrows, and perhaps acted as a temporary resting place for the dead of the community, prior to the special rites that presumably determined whether or not the individual's remains would be deposited in the long barrows, or laid in the ditches of the causewayed enclosure. However, it is also possible that the nearer causewayed

enclosure on the slopes of Overton Hill may have been the focus of these rituals, and not Windmill Hill at all. Different sectors of the community may have had allegiance to various ceremonial sites such as the long barrows. The Sanctuary therefore may have been just one of a group of special, ritual places, where the death ceremonies and temporary burial of people took place.

In its later phases, the Sanctuary probably took on a quite different character, since it was incorporated in the great Avebury complex of standing stone monuments. The stones of the Avenue and the Sanctuary appear to belong to the Beaker period, probably between 2500 and 1800 BC (2100–1500 bc). The former relationship between the Sanctuary and the causewayed enclosures probably declined at the point when the great henge at Avebury was constructed and became as the centrepiece of the whole region. The building of the West Kennet Avenue to connect Avebury with the Sanctuary reinforced the importance of the Sanctuary, and allowed the new henge to share in its status and rituals. The winding ceremonial route of the Avenue put great emphasis on the

65 *Stukeley's sketch of the Sanctuary before destruction in 1724.*

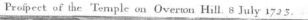

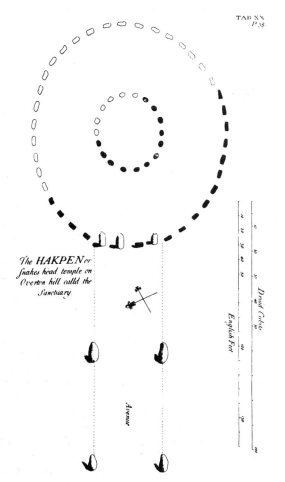

The HAKPEN or
snakes head temple on
Overton hill calld the
Sanctuary

Avenue

English Feet

Druid Cubits

TAB XX
P.38.

66 *Stukeley's plan of the Sanctuary and the beginning of the Avenue.*

prominent Sanctuary site (**colour plate 4**), and functions of both the henge and the Sanctuary became interlinked. Some writers have suggested that the henge represented fertility rituals, whereas death rituals continued to be celebrated at the Sanctuary. There is little evidence for systematic burial at Avebury, other than rare human remains in the ditches. In comparison, there is the dedicatory burial at

the Sanctuary, dating from the beginning of the stone-built phase, as well as the great number of scattered human remains in the Sanctuary.

The West Kennet Avenue

The West Kennet Avenue is the best preserved avenue in central southern England, and it may always have been the most impressive (**67,68**). It was built at a time when the later Neolithic community began to increase their manipulation of the landscape to fit specific designs. By connecting two sites of major importance, the avenue of standing stones expanded the area of ritual landscape, and thus the importance of the whole complex.

Originally, the avenue consisted of about 100 pairs of standing stones. These stones defined a corridor some 49 ft (15 m) wide along the whole of the sinuous one and a half mile (2.3 km) course. Each pair of stones stood about 80 ft (24.5 m) from the next. The sarsen stones were not as large as those used in the main circles at Avebury, for they average 10 ft (3 m) high, but range between 5 ft (1.5 m) and 14 ft (4 m). The stones appear to have been carefully selected for their shape; some are long and cylindrical, whilst others are broad and often triangular in shape. Generally stones of the two different types stood opposite each other. Keiller, following his excavations at the Avenue, suggested that they may have been intended as male and female representations, the male being long and cylindrical and the female triangular.

The line of the Avenue extends from the north-west side of the Sanctuary on Overton Hill, and then, following the line of the modern A4 road, west to the bottom of the valley, where it curves northwards, following a snaking route towards the henge on the plateau at Avebury. Little regard appears to have been taken of the natural contours, and on first sight, there seems little logic behind the choice of the course. The curving nature of the Avenue can be explained to some extent by the archaeological discover-

Table of pottery sequence and dimensions of phases at the Sanctuary

Phase	Diameter in metres	Pottery	approx. dates	
			bc	BC
1	4.5	Windmill Hill, Ebbsfleet	2500	3245
2	11.2	?Peterborough wares	2100	2670
3	20.1	Beaker, Mortlake, Grooved ware	2050	2470
4	40.2	Beaker	1800–1600	2230–1975

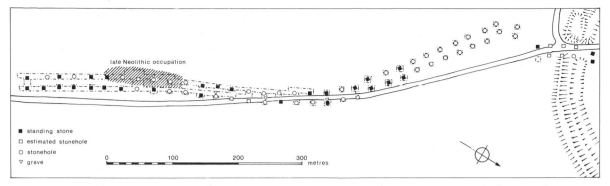

standing stone
estimated stonehole
stonehole
grave

67 *Plan of the West Kennet Avenue, showing the excavation trenches, position of the stones, Beaker graves, and the location of the later Neolithic occupation site (after Smith 1965).*

ies made by Keiller in 1934–5. Some 547 yds (500 m) from the entrance to Avebury henge, a dense scatter of later Neolithic flint and pottery was found and explored in detail. The site had the appearance of a settlement or a building of

68 *Aerial view of the West Kennet Avenue from Avebury at the base of the picture towards West Kennet village.*

some kind, with some ten holes, perhaps post holes, and two pits which contained later Neolithic pottery, flint tools, fragments of polished axes, animal bones and domestic waste and charcoal. The later Avenue appears to have been partly incorporated with the structure, since one or two stoneholes for Avenue stones could not be traced in the immediate area of the structure. The Avenue obviously curved round this building, and it is quite likely that other kinks and bends in its course also respected existing settlements and buildings.

As well as marking the route, the stones apparently also acted as grave markers for some members of the Avebury community, perhaps particularly important ones. Some time after the Avenue was erected, several burials were placed at the foot of the stones. These graves were normally shallow pits, some 3–4 ft (0.9–1.2 m) across, and at a depth of no more than 2 ft (0.6 m) below the level of the chalk. Keiller excavated four graves, all of them belonging to the Beaker period. Three of these graves contained a single individual, but the fourth had as many as three. Where the skeletons were well-preserved in two of the graves, they were found to be adult males. The grave containing three bodies had at least one adult and an adolescent (**67**).

It is possible that most burials along the Avenue were male, since in the Beaker period, the status of males appears to have become more marked, often demonstrated by the presence of rich goods in their graves such as Beaker pots, flint daggers, copper knives, bracelets, wrist guards and even items in gold. Not everyone was buried in rich graves, however, and perhaps only famous warriors or chiefs received burial in this style. Elsewhere along the Avenue, excavations revealed scatters of human bone, presumably also derived from burials, but long disturbed by allotments and the

89

burial of stones in the medieval period. The surviving burials produced some fine Beaker and Fengate pots of the later Neolithic period.

The rediscovery and excavation of the Avenue

The first record of the Avenue was made by John Aubrey in the seventeenth century, when he included a sketch of the surviving stones in his studies of Avebury. William Stukeley in the following century was fascinated by both the West Kennet and the Beckhampton Avenues, and saw the stone rows as an integral part of the great 'serpent' that he was convinced was represented by the Avebury complex (**69**). In his view the avenues formed the body of the serpent, which had its head at the Sanctuary, and its tail at the end of the very fragmentary Beckhampton Avenue. Stukeley may have been fanciful in his interpretation of the archaeological evidence, but he made a lasting record of the stones that still survived, and also gave an

69 Stukeley's plan of the 'Avebury snake' (the Avenues, Avebury and the Sanctuary).

account of the massive destruction of standing stones that was taking place during the early years of the eighteenth century. Many stones had already disappeared by the time Stukeley was recording them, and the rest were being torn down and broken into fragments for building material, often with the aid of large fires built around them. Stones had also been known to have been buried in the past, and the builders sometimes re-excavated them. Stukeley attributed the burial of the stones to farmers clearing the land for cultivation, and it was only Keiller's excavations in the 1930s which demonstrated that the stone burials had been done in the medieval period.

Throughout the nineteenth century, antiquarians became increasingly interested in Avebury, but although they speculated extensively on the course of the avenues, little actual excavation appears to have been done. When Harold St George Gray first came to Avebury to commence his excavations in 1908, he took some fine photographs of the state of the Avenue, where only four stones remained upright, and only a total of 13 stones were still visible. Maud Cunnington from the Wiltshire

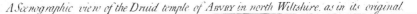

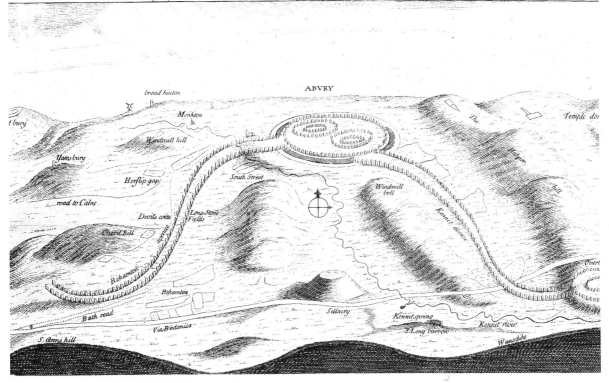

70 *Keiller's team of workmen levering a stone on the Avenue back into its original position in 1935.*

Archaeological Society undertook a small excavation when workmen digging a pipe trench unexpectedly found a buried stone on the Avenue. This was actually one of the four which produced burials in the later excavations, and was the first hint that stones still remained to be found.

Whilst engaged on his book *Wessex from the Air* with O. G. S. Crawford, Keiller bought many original Stukeley papers, some of which described Avebury and the Avenue. During his work on the Windmill Hill excavations, Keiller became more and more engrossed in the possibility that it might still be possible to find the course of the original Avenue. Stuart Piggott, his research assistant at the time, suggested that limited excavation of the probable route, coupled with information from Stukeley's archives, might reveal the position of the stones that had long since disappeared. Following his

purchase of the Avebury farm, circle, manor and avenue, Keiller commenced excavations in 1937.

Initially a parallel trench, 20 ft (6 m) wide, was opened on each side of the Avenue. This was planned to follow the course of the stone settings on each side, and buried stones and stone holes that came to light were to be examined. Work began near the main group of surviving stones at the southern end of Keiller's portion of the Avenue. As work moved closer to the Avebury circle, the late Neolithic habitation site already mentioned (p. 89) was encountered, and changed the nature of the work. However, most of the excavation was still focussed on the stones, those that still existed, those which were buried in pits, and those which were missing, and whose original position could be determined through the discovery of the stone holes in which they had been placed. Where stones survived, they were carefully levered upright (**70,71**), and then set into a shallow concrete base (**72**) to prevent them from falling again. Some of the stones had been cracked and broken by their felling in the medieval

71 *Excavations on the West Kennet Avenue in 1935, with stones being excavated and put back into position.*

period, and these were pinned together with steel rods.

Of the original 37 pairs (74 stones) that had once stood in the northern portion of the Avenue, Keiller found 13 buried stones; one stone that had become covered in hillwash; eight missing stones which had been broken using fire; and noted the positions of 30 stones which had disappeared without trace. Where stone that had become covered in hillwash; special concrete plinths designed to mark the spots, so that the full course of the restored part of the Avenue could be appreciated in full. Once Keiller had completed his restoration of the main Avenue, it was returfed, fenced, and gates were provided for visitors to gain access.

misprint

Together with Avebury stone circle, a few years later, the site was purchased with a public fund set up by Keiller, and given to the National Trust.

Keiller's former site director, W. E. V. Young, continued research on the Avenue in the 1950s, whilst he was curator of Keiller's archaeological museum at Avebury. This work was concentrated at the village of West Kennet, where the laying of drains and road widening work were thought likely to disturb more buried stones. Four more stone holes were found; the burning pit of another; and a fallen stone, still in its original position. These are now under the A4 road. The most recent development in the history of the West Kennet Avenue is that the middle portion has now been bought by the National Trust so that it too, may be preserved, and perhaps one day also investigated and restored.

92

^(?) such positions were identified

72 *A stone in the West Kennet Avenue re-set in concrete in its original position after re-erection.*

The Beckhampton Avenue

The Beckhampton Avenue now consists of only two standing stones known as Adam and Eve. When Stukeley recorded it, however, it contained about 30 stones, some still in pairs, and was about the same length as the West Kennet Avenue. Stukeley recorded stones in the High Street at Avebury, and, by linking these with other stones, he concluded that the Avenue extended beyond Adam and Eve, or the Long Stones as they are sometimes known, to a position near the Beckhampton long barrow and the roundabout on the A4 road. These plans are now kept in the Bodleian Library at Oxford.

It is still often questioned whether there was a second avenue at all. Stukeley may have recorded natural field sarsen stones, still lying in their recumbent positions, and only three of the stones he recorded were standing. However, several decades later, the curate of Avebury, Reverend Lucas recorded that an elderly parishioner, John Clements, could still point out the line of the avenue at the time of his death. This was before the two chief vandals of the standing stones, Farmer Griffin and Richard Fowler – local speculators making the most of a short-lived building boom – had destroyed the rest of the avenue. Later, even the two long stones were nearly removed by the tenant on whose land they stood, and only saved by intervention from the landlord. Stukeley thought the Long Stones represented a cove, or central setting of stones on three sides of a square, similar to that in the northern circle at Avebury. Other interpretations have suggested that the larger stone, Adam, was part of a cove or circle, and that Eve is the remains of the avenue leading to it.

Little constructive archaeological investigation has been attempted on the Beckhampton Avenue since Stukeley's time. Various stones have been recorded in gardens, bridges and in fields. Faith Vatcher, curator of the Avebury Museum during the 1960s and 1970s, kept a close eye on all drainage works and new building along the course of the avenue, and recorded several possible stones or stone holes. The extent and the complexity of the avenue still remains to be confirmed, and future investigations may well reveal its true extent.

The location and extent of the Sanctuary, on the other hand, was confirmed by excavation in 1930. Maud Cunnington of the Wiltshire Archaeological Society studied Stukeley's description of the Sanctuary with great care and excavated a long trench across part of Overton Hill, until she encountered several stone-holes left from long-destroyed standing stones. With a small team of workers, the site was excavated with trenches following the various concentric rings (63) of post-holes and stone-holes. The technique of excavation was not ideal, since the site was not stripped and studied as a whole. The trenches were filled as soon as the holes had been planned and recorded. Nevertheless, the excavation was adequate for its time, although much inferior to the precision of Keiller's excavation.

The site is still mysterious, since we know nothing of the areas of the site between Cunnington's trenches, and nothing about the areas surrounding the circles. There are no radiocarbon dates as yet, and like all the Avebury monuments its original role remains unknown, although, as Samuel Pepys speculated when he saw the stone circle in the 1660s, it was undoubtedly an elaborate building of great size and prominence.

7

Silbury Hill

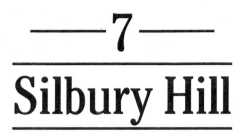

Silbury Hill is one of the most enigmatic and mysterious Neolithic sites in Europe (**colour plate 5**). It is the largest man-made mound in Europe, and rivals some of the smaller Egyptian pyramids at Giza, or the great Indian mounds of Cahokia in the USA in size. It dates from about 2700 BC and is of comparable age to the pyramids, but that is where any similarity must end. Silbury Hill is unique and still unexplained. Excavations, theories and intuitive speculations have all failed to produce definitive answers for the function of Silbury, and it seems more than likely that there will never be any archaeological breakthrough which can tell us why the site was built. However,

73 *Aerial view of Silbury looking north west. The two chalk causeways linking Silbury with the natural hillslope can be clearly seen on the road side of the hill.*

researches carried out to date have afforded a good deal of information about how the site was built and with what material and manpower. These are of great interest in themselves, and tell us much about how later Neolithic society at Avebury must have operated.

The base of Silbury Hill is almost circular, and covers an area of $5\frac{1}{4}$ acres (2.2 ha). The hill is 130 ft (40 m) high, and contains about $12\frac{1}{2}$ million cubic ft (0.35 million cubic metres) of chalk and soil. Around it was a ditch, now silted up, that was originally 16 ft (4.9 m) deep, 70 ft (21 m) wide and some 6 million cubic ft (0.17 million cubic metres) of soil and chalk was excavated to form it. Silbury Hill was not the product of a single operation; the mound we see today was built in three stages, each of these making the hill grander and more impressive than the last. Traces of these early stages were discovered in 1968–9, when with sponsorship from the BBC, Richard Atkinson led a Cardiff University team of archaeologists to excavate a tunnel to the very centre of the mound (**74, colour plate 6**). Although not the first excavation, (there had been numerous others since 1776), the Atkinson project had precise and attainable goals. These were to take samples of soil, seeds, animal remains and preserved wood for study. The information retrieved has been of great interest, allowing us to understand how and when Silbury Hill was built.

The first phase of construction
The first phase of work began in late summer, perhaps in August, when most of the crops had been harvested, and people would have had time to spend on building works. At a time when the ants were just beginning to grow wings and fly away from their anthills in the turf, a circle

74 *Professor Richard Atkinson lifts the first spade of turf at the beginning of the 1968 excavation of Silbury Hill, amidst a blaze of publicity.*

about 120 ft (36.6 m) in diameter was staked out on a small projection of the hillslope, beside the River Kennett, and gravel from the Kennett stream was heaped in a thick layer. Then turves, still full of ants whose remains have survived, were stacked up and enclosed within the now closely staked-out area. Following this, four consecutive layers of soil, clay, chalk and gravel were collected from the immediate area. These were each about 2 ft (0.6 m) thick, and each

material had a distinctive colour from the one below and above. In appearance this first mound must have looked rather like a drum, 15 ft (4.5 m) high, (**75**), but it was not left like this for long.

The second phase of construction

This time, the structure was to be conical in shape, and work commenced with the excavation of a large ditch to enclose the existing mound. It was about 40 ft (12 m) wide and 20 ft (6 m) deep, and enclosed a circle of 350 ft (107 m) in diameter, double the size of the drum-

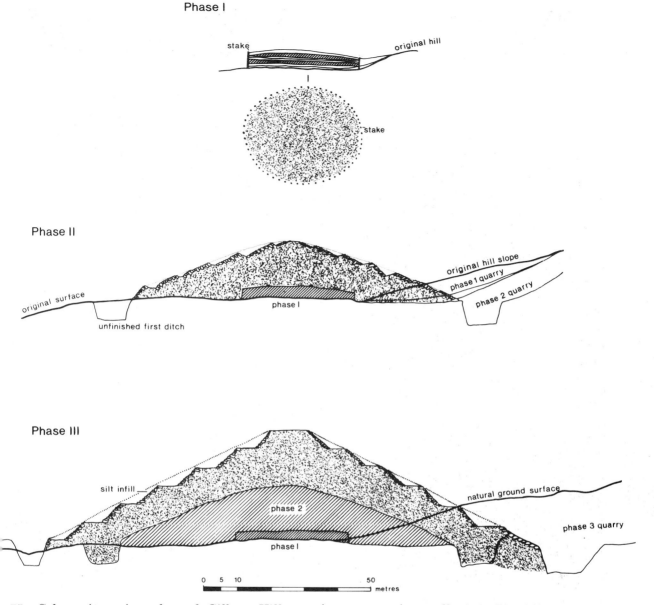

Phase I

stake   original hill

stake

Phase II

original surface
unfinished first ditch
phase I
original hill slope
phase 1 quarry
phase 2 quarry

Phase III

silt infill
phase 2
phase I
natural ground surface
phase 3 quarry

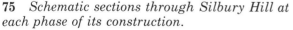

0   5 10   50
                                      metres

75 *Schematic sections through Silbury Hill at each phase of its construction.*

shaped mound at the centre. The site now clipped the end of the chalk hillside on the south, which was utilised as a chalk quarry for the construction of two chalk causeways, linking the hillside to Silbury. These can still be seen today (**73**). The second hill was built largely of chalk blocks, amounting to about 1 million cubic feet (0.028 million cubic metres). These were carefully built into sloping steps, and held together by an intricate network of interconnecting walls (**76**). The hill probably reached a height of about 55 ft (16.7 m), but it is impossible to know quite what it looked like. The surrounding ditch was never fully completed, and ideas of increased grandeur appear to have halted work before the second hill was finished.

The third phase of construction
Even before the surrounding ditch was completed, the builders changed their plans yet again. The third phase of Silbury was even more splendid than the second, and involved

97

76 *Diagram showing the interior chalk wall construction of Silbury Hill.*

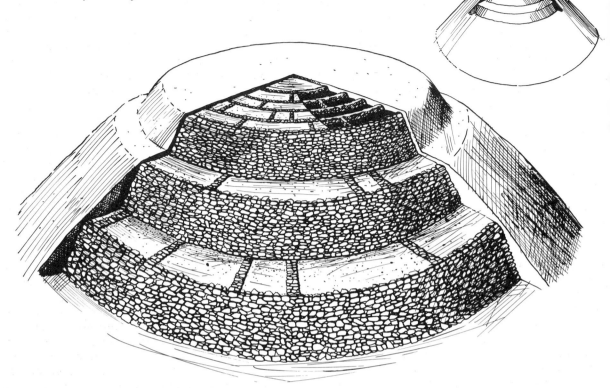

77 *The chalk walls under excavation in 1969–70 at the top of Silbury.*

the enlargement of the whole scheme, and the construction of a third layer of artificial hill over the first two phases, completely enveloping the earlier mounds. The first ditch was filled in again, and another, even larger ditch was excavated to provide more chalk, and to surround the site (**73**).

This second ditch was cut outside the earlier one, and now covered a diameter of about 380 ft (116 m) on its inner face. It was over 20 ft (6 m) deep, and 70 ft (21 m) wide. The new mound imitated the exact profile of phase 2, and was also angled at a steady 30 degrees. It was formed from six concentric steps, each about 15–17 ft high, one on top of the other. These were also formed from chalk blocks, and built in the same honeycomb fashion as the second phase, each step leaning slightly inwards, and forming a remarkably stable structure (**77**). Each of the chalk cells formed by the walls was infilled with a mix of chalk rubble and silt. In order to obtain enough chalk, the quarry around the base of Silbury, begun in the second phase, was enlarged by a further $2\frac{1}{2}$ acres (1 ha), emphasizing the man-made hill even more than before, through the exaggerated profile of the hillside. Even the new quarry cannot have provided all the chalk needed to build the hill, and other areas around must have been exploited. In total, the hill required a further $6\frac{1}{2}$ million cubic ft (0.18 million cubic metres) of chalk, soil and stone to enlarge it after the second phase, to a total of $12\frac{1}{2}$ million cubic ft (0.35 million cubic metres) of man-made hill. Only the bottom 30 ft (9 m) of the hill was formed from the natural hillslope, and the rest of the structure was the result of the carefully-designed construction described above. The hill covers a total of $5\frac{1}{2}$ acres (2 ha) and has a diameter of about 520 ft (159 m).

The purpose of Silbury Hill

When one looks at the enormous effort which went into the construction of Silbury Hill, the overwhelming impression is that the site must have been of major importance to its builders. What, then, was it intended for, and why did such colossal effort go into making it?

The date at which Silbury was begun can be determined from the turves found at the very base of the hill, and which have been dated by radio-carbon to around 2800–2600 BC (2200 bc) which is the period of transition between the middle and later Neolithic period, a time when massive social changes appear to have been taking place. As far as we can judge, at this time society was beginning to stratify into a hierarchy, with the emergence of some individuals more influential and powerful than the rest. It was also a period when agriculture was becoming more diverse, with perhaps a split between farmers and shepherds, traders and craftsmen, and also a transformation in settlement patterns reflecting these other changes. In the case of Silbury, it seems likely that the decision to build the hill was made by a small group of people, or even by one influential leader alone. Silbury Hill is the single most impressive engineering feat of prehistoric Britain, in terms of the amount of human effort needed to build it. Stonehenge probably required greater architectural skills, but still required only a small portion of the time spent on Silbury. It has been calculated that 3,000,000 man-hours (perhaps 700 men working for ten years) were invested in the digging and transportation of chalk and soil, and that perhaps the various phases of the site took decades, if not centuries, to complete (**colour plate 7**).

There are numerous theories about the meaning and the function of Silbury Hill, some outlandish, and others more acceptable to modern archaeological views. The traditional explanation of Silbury was that the mound was a great tomb, that of the legendary King Sel, who was buried, according to William Stukeley's researches, with his horse and a complete set of gold armour. Another popular view is that Silbury represents a mother goddess, where the mound is symbolic of the pregnant womb. However, this theory rests much of its argument on an aerial view of the site and on comparison with goddess figurines from distant parts of the world, neither of which would have been available to Neolithic people. Ley-line theories are also popular, with Silbury as part of a great line of power linking other sites, including Avebury and Stonehenge. However, ley-line theories depend on straight lines, and none of the Avebury monuments have these, curves and circles predominating instead.

More valid speculation on its function has focussed on how such an edifice related to the remainder of the Avebury monuments. The mound is high, and yet it is not visible from every direction; in particular it cannot be seen from within the Avebury circles. Indeed, had the builders really wanted the site to have been

78 *Atkinson standing at the bottom of the final Silbury Ditch during excavations in 1969.*

visible from afar, they would have built it on high ground, not in the lowest area of the upper Kennett valley. So if the site was not intended as a great landmark, what was it for? Investigations have failed to reveal anything within the mound, such as a burial or a symbolic hoard or shrine, and it therefore seems likely that the mound was important in itself, not for what it contained. The actual site may have been chosen for some symbolic reason, perhaps where a battle was won or a great warrior was killed, or it may have marked either the boundary or the centre of the territory of an influential chief.

Other comparable sites are known in the area; the now ruined Marlborough mound (**79**), and the great barrow site that once existed within the henge at Marden in the Vale of Pewsey. Both these artificial hills were located, like Silbury, beside streams; indeed the Marlborough mound is a mere 5 miles (8 km) east of this point on the same Kennett river. It was excavated in the last century, and revealed antler picks, just like the Neolithic examples

79 *Aerial view of the Marlborough Mound, another Neolithic edifice, in the grounds of Marlborough College, now sadly anonymous beneath its cover of trees.*

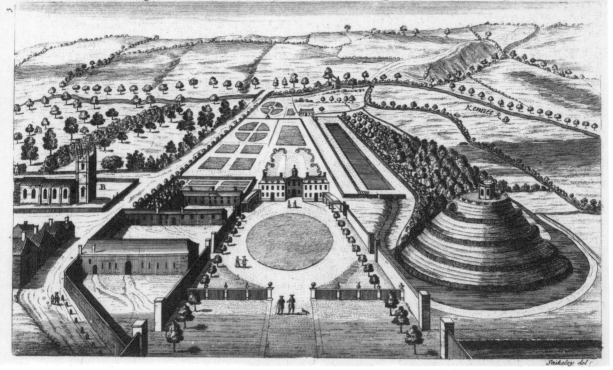

B. S. Peters. *View of Lord* Hartfords House *at* Marlborough 29 Iun. 1723. A. *the Scite of the Roman Castrum*

Stukeley del.

80 *Stukeley's sketch of the Marlborough Mound in 1723 when it supported an elegant hanging garden and grotto.*

from Avebury and Silbury. However, the site is much ruined, having been terraced as a hanging garden in the eighteenth century (**80**), and more recently overgrown by large trees and used for the site of a large water tank. The barrow in the Marden henge was excavated by Richard Colt Hoare and his assistant Cunnington in the early years of the nineteenth century. They were searching for a burial, which they failed to find, and the barrow, apparently constructed mainly of sand, fell apart as they dug. Now even the site of the mound can be located only through geophysical survey methods. Cunnington recorded that the barrow was of vast size, very much larger than any on Salisbury Plain, and it seems probable in the context of its position in the henge that it was an unusual Neolithic construction, not dissimilar to Silbury and its position in the Avebury landscape.

In the context of the vast Avebury complex, Silbury Hill becomes more understandable than it would in most other locations. The Neolithic landscape includes the largest causewayed enclosure, the most complex and massive henge, the two longest long barrows in Wessex, the longest Avenue, and, perhaps, logically, the largest man-made mound in Europe.

Subsequent history and investigation of Silbury Hill

After the great period of Neolithic Avebury, which perhaps ended around 1800 BC, the ritual landscape gradually fell into disuse. The Bronze Age population do not appear to have paid much attention to the complex, and instead concentrated on building their individual round barrows on all the hilltops and open areas around the upper Kennett valley. The Iron Age people also seem to have paid no attention to Silbury. The Romans exploited the site in a novel way, using it for sighting their new road from Mildenhall to Bath. This road can still be seen preserved west of Avebury, and can be picked out clearly on aerial photographs (**8**). The Roman engineers probably stood on the summit of Silbury and sighted the new road both east and west. At Silbury itself, the road had to make an unexpected kink, linking the two straight sections on either side. In the Saxon period, the hill appears to have become a lookout post, and it is possible that the summit was fortified. It is even possible that the top step of the hill, which has usually been interpreted as a Neolithic feature, was actually re-excavated, so that the lookout at the top had a lower tier of fortification. Certainly the excavations in 1968–9 showed the whole top area to be disturbed, perhaps both from Saxon fortification and from the work of earlier antiquaries.

The first record of Silbury was made by John Aubrey. He brought Charles II to see Avebury in 1663, and at the same time 'his majesty cast his eie on Silsbury Hill about a mile off: which they had the curiosity to see, and walkt to the top of it with Duke of Yorke, Dr Charlton and I attending them'. Aubrey sketched the hill in his plans of Avebury and the West Kennet Avenue. He attempted to discover what the hill was through local researches, and his general conclusion, like those of most other antiquaries after him, was that the hill contained a great tomb. He wrote that 'no history gives any account of this hill. The tradition only is that King Sel or Zel, as the country folk pronounce,

was buried here on horseback, and that the hill was raysed while a posset of milk was seething.' Not long after Aubrey described Silbury, Samuel Pepys, travelling past on the road to Bath, stopped and learned from local labourers that 'one King Seall [was] buried there, as tradition says'.

The next notable record of the hill was made by William Stukeley, the eighteenth-century antiquarian who recorded so much of the surviving Neolithic Avebury landscape before it was destroyed by local builders. Although his main preoccupation was the great stones at Avebury and the two avenues (see Chapter 9), Silbury Hill became a crucial part of his theories about Avebury. From 1723, when Stukeley learnt that workmen had discovered decayed bones, an iron knife with a bone handle, deer antlers and a rusty horse bit in the superficial soil at the top of the mound when planting trees, he accepted that the hill was prehistoric, and therefore older than the workmen's find and older than Avebury itself. He also thought that it must be a tomb. 'Silbury is indeed the most astonishing collection of earth, artificially raised, worthy of the king who was the royal founder of Abury as we may plausibly affirm... by considering the picture of Abury temple, we may discern,

81 *Stukeley's sketch of Silbury in 1723. Stukeley recognized the Roman road (now the A4) passing the hill on the south side.*

Silbury Hill *July 11. 1723.*

A. *The Roman road.* B. *the Snakes head or hakpen.*

that as this immense body of earth was rais'd for the sake of the interment of the great Prince, whoever he was: for the temple of Abury was made for the sake of this tumulus; and then I have no sample (*sic*) to affirm, 'tis the most magnificent mausoleum in the world, without excepting the Egyptian Pyramids.' These observations were quite sensible, but by the time Stukeley had dwelt on his theories for a further twenty years, his interpretation of Silbury in 1743 was as follows: 'Silbury stands exactly south of Abury, the head and tail of the snake. The work of Abury, which is the circle and the two Avenues which represent the snake transmitted thro' it and the... sacred prophylactic character of the divine mind, which is to protect the depositum of the Prince here interred.' What was worse, he tangled up these theories with others involving druids, and managed to include them together with his snake, circle and ancient Egyptians, into a bizarre explanation for the whole Avebury complex.

After Stukeley, there were no other particularly interesting accounts of Silbury until the first excavation of the hill took place. This was done by a team of Cornish tin miners for the Duke of Northumberland in 1776. A tunnel was driven from the top of the hill, straight down to the base, where the Duke, a typical eighteenth-century dilettante, hoped to find antiques and a fabulous ancient tomb, with which he might furnish his home. He was disappointed, for nothing was found but a fragment of oak timber.

Throughout the nineteenth century, with a growing interest in archaeology, Silbury attracted much interest. However, without further investigation of its interior, little more could be learnt. In 1849, the Archaeological Institute, under the direction of the engineer Henry Blandford, and the archaeologically-minded Dean Mereweather of Hereford, undertook another tunnelling exercise. This time, a tunnel was put through from the side, and after digging through 100 feet of solid chalk, in a tunnel $6\frac{1}{2}$ ft (2.0 m) high, and 3 ft (0.9 m) wide, the old soil surface was reached at the centre of the mound. However, no burial chamber was found, and the Institute had to content itself with an inconclusive project. They left behind them, however, a cache of small mementos, including newspaper cuttings of 1849, an almanack, posters and a poem, all packed carefully in a sealed jar. This came to light during the 1968–9 excavations, under the scrutiny of television cameras.

A more practical project was carried out in 1867, when the Wiltshire Archaeological Society decided to test the theory that the hill was more ancient than the Roman road that appeared to skirt around the base. An excavation was opened at the side of the hill, at the point where the road should have gone underneath, had it been earlier than Silbury. The theory proved to be correct, and no trace of the Roman road was found running beneath the hill.

In 1886, a further project was undertaken. This time, ten exploratory shafts were dug around the north and west sides of the hill, in an attempt to find the ancient landsurface, and to examine the make-up of the hill. These holes proved that the water-table was 8 ft (2.4 m) below, and that the original ground surface was between 16 and 20 feet (4.8–6 m) below the present ground level.

These investigations satisfied curiosity for some years, until in 1922 Sir Flinders Petrie, the famous archaeologist who had returned from excavating in Egypt, decided to make another investigation. He excavated a tunnel opposite the east causeway, where he imagined the formal entrance to the great tomb should be. However, it soon became apparent that there was no entrance, and instead layer upon layer of horizontally laid soil and chalk. Disappointed, but maintaining an academic interest in the site, Petrie re-opened the 1849 tunnel and explored part of the passage. The entrance to the tunnel had fallen down in 1915, but until then it had been accessible. After Petrie's work, the tunnel was sealed properly in 1923 by the Office of Works. These efforts seem to have quenched any further desire to explore Silbury until more scientific archaeology offered alternative methods of examining the mysterious site.

The 1968 project was carried out under the bright lights of publicity. The project was sponsored by the BBC, and undertaken principally by Cardiff University. Mining students were used to open a tunnel, very close to the mouth of the 1849 one and angled so that it would follow the original tunnel, after avoiding an area of known collapse near the entrance. The Department of Geography at Bristol University had previously surveyed the site. Then the Nature Conservation Board made a very detailed study of the flora of the hill. The Zoology Department of Southampton University studied the local animal life, and the Geology Department from Cardiff experimented with geophysical remote survey techniques, including making borings through the mound, and using echo-sounding equipment to discover the depth of the great buried ditch. The excavations succeeded in reaching the centre of the hill after a period of some six weeks' work, and a length of some 77 yds (70 m) of the mound base and buried ground level were exposed in continuous section. This was then studied in detail, and samples of each layer of soil, chalk, buried wood, and buried turf were taken for analysis. The preservation of organic remains was extraordinarily good, and the turf was quite recognizable as grass, with even its greenish colour being preserved. From a study of the long section through the layers, the three different phases of Silbury became apparent, with the small first mound with its wooden stakes surrounding it, followed by the much larger second mound with its ditch, and finally the last phase – Silbury as it still remains.

The press clearly hoped that a spectacular burial would be unearthed, and until the moment when the centre was reached, television coverage hovered hopefully for the great moment which never came. For archaeologists and palaeoenvironmentalists, however, the finds within the hill were more than sufficient to justify the effort that had gone into the project, since the building phases of Silbury were at last known, and remarkable environmental and dating samples had been recovered, showing that the environment of Silbury was not so unlike that still surviving on its flanks today. The ingenuity of the prehistoric builders was at last appreciated, and precise estimates about how long and how much material had gone into the structure could be calculated. But in spite of the discovery of these remarkable details about the hill, the failure to find a tomb resulted in a curtailment of the project, and a general lack of interest thereafter in publishing its results. Some excavation continued in 1970, after the BBC had withdrawn support, to explore the outside of the hill. It was found that the hill was made up, as described above, of interlinked walls of chalk, constructed in six consecutive steps, holding the site together. The steps had been filled in with locally-collected silt (**77**).

8
The construction of the Great Henge

The Avebury henge is one of the largest and undoubtedly the most complex of all the stone circles surviving today. It was probably always one of the premier henge sites of Neolithic Britain, and, as we have seen from the preceding chapters, represented the climax of the whole Avebury complex.

The henge compares in size to the much simpler enclosures of Marden, Durrington Walls and Mount Pleasant, but when its actual proportions are compared, Avebury was a far more elaborate and labour intensive monument than

82 *Aerial view of Avebury on a misty evening looking west.*

the others. Its massive bank and ditch alone stand out as monumentally vast, particularly so in comparison to the bank and ditch at Stonehenge. The number and size of the stones erected in the circle is also unparalleled, with an estimated minimum of 247 standing stones within the circle, and a further 97 pairs of standing stones making up the West Kennet Avenue.

The outer ditch with its bank enclosed an area of 28½ acres (11.5 ha), with a mean internal diameter of 1140 ft (347.4 m). The shape formed by the ditch is not a perfect circle, but instead a curiously amorphous 'D' shape, divided by causewayed entrances into four unequal arcs. No amount of clever geometry or astro-archaeological theorising can really pretend that the Neolithic builders had sophisticated survey equipment at their disposal. The great monument has all the appearance of having been paced out roughly on the ground. After that, teams of workers excavated the ditch, probably starting at different points, and meeting, somewhat haphazardly, on the way. The site chosen was the highest point on a slightly dome-shaped rise in the flattish area of Avebury. The highest point lies near the centre, more or less on the site of the modern Red Lion Inn. All the ground slopes away from there towards the outer ditch and bank.

The ditch, although now silted to more than halfway up its original depth (**83**) was once between 23 and 33 ft (7–10 m) in depth, with a width at its top edge of some 70 ft (23.4 m), and a square-bottomed base, which averaged about

105

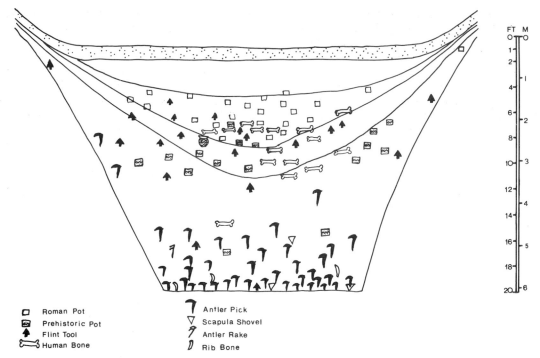

☐ Roman Pot	⌐	Antler Pick
⊠ Prehistoric Pot	▽	Scapula Shovel
♠ Flint Tool	⌐	Antler Rake
⟋⟍ Human Bone	⌐	Rib Bone

83 *Section through the ditch of the henge at Avebury, showing the stratified layers, with Neolithic material well sealed beneath later Roman rubbish.*

84 *Section through the great henge ditch, showing the stratified layers, as excavated by H. St George Gray 1908-22.*

13 ft (3.9 m) across. In the north-west sector of the circle, the ditch was dug through the lower chalk, and in the other sections through both the middle and lower chalk. In some of the stone holes of the standing stones, lower chalk was encountered as packing material, clearly indicating that these stones were erected in association with the digging of the ditch. The bank was formed from the material that was

excavated and mounded up outside the ditch, an unusual arrangement. The bank is about 4440 ft or four-fifths of a mile (1353 m; 1.3 km) in length. The height is now some 14–18 ft (4.2–5.4 m) above the ground level of the circle, but was originally some 55 ft (16.7 m) above what was originally a 30-ft (9 m) deep ditch. The width of the bank was between 75-100 ft (22.8–30.4 m) and the whole edifice must have been a spectacular sight in stark white chalk when first erected.

The bank is as irregular as the ditch in shape, and appears to have been built by different work gangs. There was originally a flat area

85 *Plan of Avebury as it may have been during the final Neolithic period (after Smith 1965).*

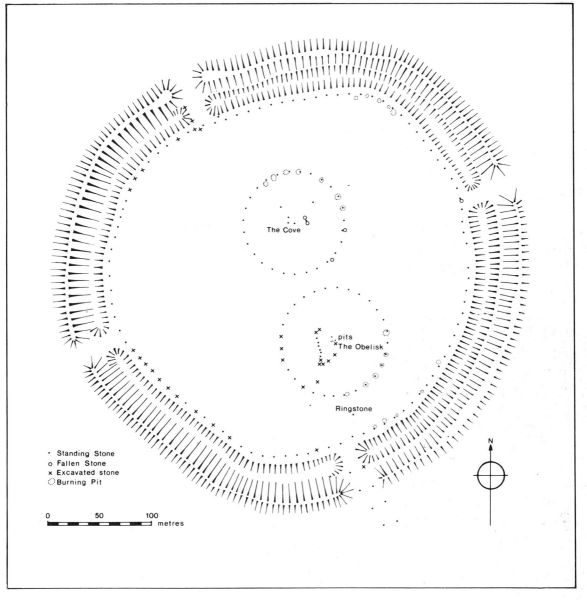

The Cove

pits
The Obelisk

Ringstone

- Standing Stone
o Fallen Stone
x Excavated stone
◌ Burning Pit

0   50   100
        metres

N

(the berm) between the inner base of the bank and the top outer edge of the ditch. Chalk walling consisting of lower chalk blocks quarried from the base of the ditch had edged the inner edge of the bank in places, presumably to prevent the chalk and soil slipping rapidly back into the ditch. Where the bank ended at a causeway, timber revetments appear to have been used to keep the bank in place. The surfaces of the four causewayed entrances had been reduced by scraping the top layers of chalk, so that the banks at either side appeared even higher and more impressive. There may also have been timber entrances of some kind, restricting access to the circles to only a few people at a time. Together with the stones, the great henge at Avebury took many hundreds

of thousands of man-hours to complete. It was the second most labour-intensive Neolithic monument in Britain after Silbury Hill.

The building of the circles

There are three great stone circles at Avebury, an outer circle of some 98 very large stones placed just inside the ditch, and two smaller inner circles which were aligned more or less north and south. The northern circle has the Cove at its centre, which was originally a three-sided arrangement of huge stones. In the southern circle a single high stone, later called the Obelisk, was the dominant feature.

The actual sequence of construction of the circles is not well understood, but it is quite likely that before the main outer and even the inner stone circles were erected, timber circles and buildings, as at the other Wessex henges, may have originally filled the area within the bank. Some stones have been shown to belong

86 *Stone setting, known as the 'Z' feature, around the site of the Obelisk in the southern circle at Avebury (after Smith 1965).*

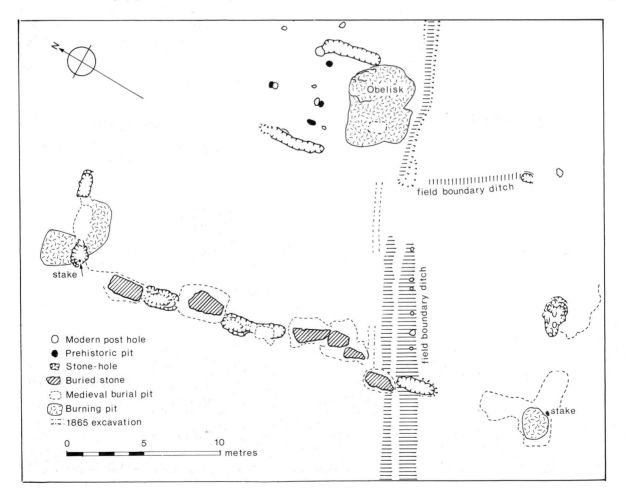

Legend:
- O Modern post hole
- ● Prehistoric pit
- Stone-hole
- Buried stone
- Medieval burial pit
- Burning pit
- 1865 excavation

0   5   10 metres

to an arrangement quite separate from the geometrically-placed stones in the circles. These may be remnants of earlier settings, possibly contemporary with the digging of the ditch, and perhaps served quite different functions, such as lining up with other stones, or even with the sun or moon. The two inner circles were laid out with almost perfect precision within the Great Circle. One stood to the north of centre circle, and the other to the south, each having a different arrangement of stones and pits. Both the inner circles were large in comparison to other later Neolithic examples, the southern circle having a radius of 170 ft (51 m) and the northern circle one of 160 ft (48.7 m). The whole of Stonehenge having a radius of only 97 ft (29.5 m) could have comfortably fitted within either of these, and this fact alone makes it clear that Avebury is in a class of its own.

The southern circle focused on its central point, the great Obelisk, which was the tallest stone in the circle, some 21 ft (6.4 m) in height, and 8ft 9 in (2.7 m) in diameter. It was sur-

rounded by 29 smaller standing stones, which formed the circle. These were regularly set at intervals of about 36 ft (10.9 m), which is the same as the stones in the outer circle. The heights of the stones were also similar to those in the outer circle, varying from 9–13 ft (2.7–3.9 m). Around the central point of the Obelisk, an arrangement of smaller rough sarsen stones formed a near-rectangular enclosure which had already been staked out with wooden posts. When excavated this curious alignment was called the 'Z' feature. South of it was a single stone, perhaps lining up with the southern causewayed entrance. Just to the north of the Obelisk, four pits were excavated into the chalk, to a depth of 1–1.5 ft (.30–.45 m). These may have had a special function associated with the ceremonial activities in the circle, and were filled with clean soil before any rubbish could fall down them.

The northern circle probably consisted of 27 stones, also spaced at the interval used elsewhere at Avebury of about 36 ft (10.9 m). Most of the original stones are now missing, but two still stand, and two more lie on the ground. At the centre is the remains of the Cove, or the Devil's Brandirons, as it was popularly

87 *Stukeley's sketch of the northern circle at Avebury.*

A View of the Remains of the Northern Temple at Abury. Aug. 1722.

A. Abury Steeple. B. the cove. C. Windmill hill.

88 *Reconstruction sketch of the Neolithic excavation of the Avebury ditch (Judith Dobie).*

known (**colour plate 11**). This once consisted of three vast sarsen stones, rectangular in shape, arranged around three sides of a square, with the opening to the north. The stones were some of the largest used at Avebury, ranging from 16 ft high by 8 ft wide (4.8 × 2.4 m), to 14 ft high by 16 ft wide (4.2 × 4.8 m). The missing stone (which fell in 1713) was alleged by Stukeley to be 'seven yards long', so it too may have been about 16 ft (4.8 m) high. Although not visible today, it is likely that, like the Obelisk in the southern circle, the Cove was surrounded by rows or a ring of smaller sarsen stones. There were also outlying stones within the northern circle, which may have been aligned with other stones, causewayed entrances or even simple astronomical sightings.

The main outer circle at Avebury probably had 98 stones arranged around the perimeter edge of the surrounding ditch. The stones were quite variable in shape and size. The tallest ones (around 14 ft (4.2 m) high) stood at the northern and southern entrances to the henge,

89 *Neolithic transport of the Avebury sarsen stones may have been on wooden rollers with teams of people dragging the stones (Judith Dobie).*

presumably placed to form impressive openings into the large circle of the henge. The shapes chosen, like the stones of the West Kennet Avenue, were of two main types, long, column-shaped stones where the height of the stone far exceeded the breadth, and a second triangular-shaped type, where the breadth often exceeded the height. The stones at the southern and northern entrances were of this latter type, and the great Swindon stone at the north entrance typifies the triangular shape.

The number of people involved in the building of Avebury was probably not as great as Silbury Hill, but nevertheless the digging of the vast ditch and the transportation of the stones was a tremendous feat of simple engineering and of the organization of manpower. The volume of chalk dug from the ditch was about half that required to build Silbury, but it all had to be quarried through middle and lower chalk. Silbury contained a volume of about 9 million cubic ft (0.25 million cubic metres), whereas the ditch at Avebury had 4 million cubic ft (0.12 million cubic metres) of chalk excavated and then mounded up to form the bank. It has been estimated that something between 650,000 and 1,540,000 man-hours must have been invested in the ditch excavation and the transportation and erection of the sarsen stones.

The stones that made up the main circles at Avebury were some of the largest natural

sarsens from the surrounding hills and valleys. They were carefully selected, and possibly some had to be partly excavated from the surrounding silts and soils within which they were naturally buried. None of the stone was shaped artificially, unlike the Stonehenge sarsens, but all of them were selected for both shape and size. Most of the stones probably came from the Marlborough Downs, where large sarsens were worked for building stone until the last century, although some may have been more local to Avebury, from the Kennett valley.

Once selected, teams of people armed only with wooden sledges and rollers and leather straps shifted the massive stones by rolling or pulling them along (89). Although averaging about 15 tons (15.2 tonnes) in weight, some of

90 *An experiment on the West Kennet Avenue: levering a fallen stone upright in its original hole.*

the larger stones weighed between 20 and 60 tons (20.3 and 61.0 tonnes), (the great Swindon stone is estimated to weigh about 63.5 tons (64.5 tonnes) and must have presented many problems both in their transportation to Avebury, and in setting them upright in position. An experiment conducted in 1934, when raising one of the Avenue stones, showed that each stone took a considerable time to raise into position. The stone in the Avenue only measured 8.8 × 6.4 × 1.6 ft (2.6 × 1.9 × 0.48 m), and took 12 untrained men with two foremen four days to raise vertical using only wood levers and steel cables (**90**). We may conclude that even if they were more practised at it, the Avebury builders required several days just to raise each stone into position.

When the stones were brought to the henge, they do not appear to have been systematically placed in position respecting either shape or

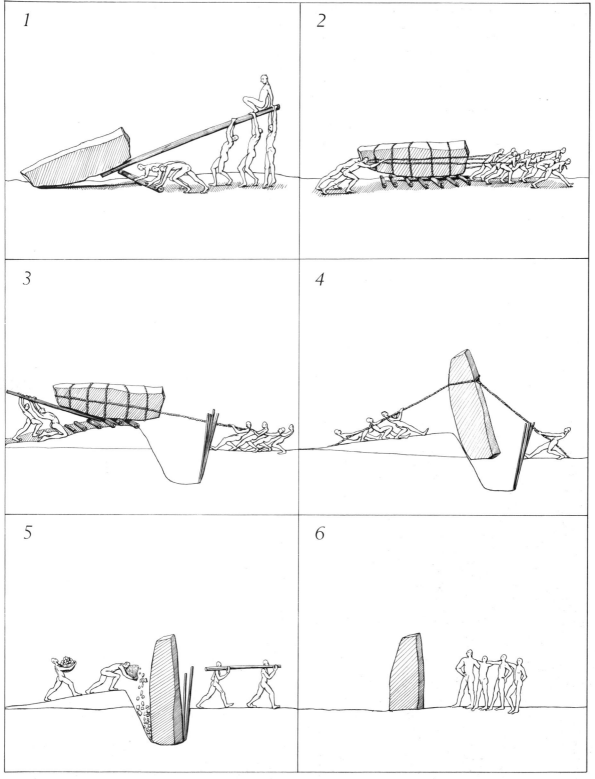

91 *Diagram of a possible method of raising a stone in Neolithic Avebury (Judith Dobie).*

size, unlike the West Kennet Avenue, where stones were paired according to shape (column-shaped opposite triangular). Only the massive stones at the entrance were specially selected, with the Swindon stone at the north entrance (and its now missing twin) and the two Portal stones at the south entrance representing very large versions of the triangular-shaped stones. However, the shapes of stones in the main circles do conform to the two types, and there may once have been more patterning in their arrangement than is now possible for us to reconstruct.

Once the stones were dragged into their approximate position, a small, shallow hole was excavated to about 3–4 ft (0.9–1.2 m) into the chalk where the stone was to stand. Then small stakes were set in a curving line on the side opposite the stone on its rollers, so that when the stone was raised into position with wood props, levers, ropes and the strength of many people, the stakes would prevent friction, and stop the stone toppling forward. Other wood posts and stakes were used to guide the stone into its hole, in an attempt to prevent it skewing. The ground between the hole and the stone may sometimes have been made into a low soil ramp to assist in the lifting and tipping of the stone. Once the stone was in position and held by wood props and ropes, packing material of clay, chalk blocks, small sarsen stones and flints was used to secure it in the hole. Each stone was carefully positioned so that its centre of gravity was directly over the stone hole (**colour plate 10**).

The standing stones at Avebury represent one of the great building feats of prehistoric Britain. Altogether the great circles included a minimum of some 247 stones, and the two avenues may have been composed of a further 300–400 stones, each weighing several tons Stonehenge, the only site comparable with Avebury, had over 40 standing sarsen stones, with a further 34 lintels raised to form the trilithons, and over 60 smaller bluestones. The sarsens had been dragged over a greater distance from the Marlborough Downs and had been shaped with stone hammers to form smooth profiles, so the investment of time and effort at Stonehenge may not have been very different from Avebury. But Avebury was at the centre of one of the best natural stone sources in Wessex, and it is understandable that the sarsen stone was exploited early in the

Neolithic occupation of the area with its use in the chambered barrows. Elsewhere in southern Britain, would-be Neolithic architects had to be content with timber constructions, or small boulders or earth banks arranged in circles and alignments to achieve the impressive ceremonial monuments they wanted. Clearly few places were able to compete with the impressive stones of Avebury, and it is significant that the main sarsen circle at Stonehenge followed the Avebury constructions by several hundred years, being built around 2000–1800 BC.

Avebury was not the only circle of standing stones in the area of the Kennett valley, but was the centre point of several smaller, satellite circles. As Avebury was a major ceremonial and cult centre, it is quite likely that the smaller circles were used for associated activities, perhaps of a more specialized nature, and perhaps by different sections of society.

The nearest circle was the Faulkner ring, which lay to the east of the West Kennet Avenue. One stone still survives in the hedge of a cornfield, but originally the circle consisted of about a dozen stones, and was associated with a nearby Bronze Age round barrow. The circle, which has never been investigated archaeologically, may date from the early Bronze Age, or the Beaker period. Whatever the activities were that went on this circle, they must have been closely associated with those of the West Kennet Avenue.

The western end of the Beckhampton Avenue probably also ended in a stone circle, and even though William Stukeley thought it lay west of the Long Stones, it is more likely that the Long Stones represented a stone circle with a Cove at its centre. Such a circle might have mirrored in miniature the stone circle of the Sanctuary in its final phases at the end of the West Kennet Avenue.

The Ridgeway path was important in the location of other stone circles. Only a few hundred yards north of the Sanctuary on Overton Hill was a small stone circle, lying just west of the Ridgeway. This had been all but destroyed by the time Stukeley studied the Sanctuary in the early eighteenth century. About a mile to the south of the Sanctuary, on the high ground at Cow Down, and also just west of the Ridgeway, was a small, fairly rough circle, called the Langdene Circle, amongst a dense area of sarsen stones. This is now almost impossible to distinguish, and has never been investigated archaeologically. Another small rustic circle is located about 3 miles (4.8 km) north of the Sanctuary, also just west of the Ridgeway, on the edge of Manton Down amongst dense scatters of natural sarsen stones. It too has never been investigated. The remains of a small circle also survive about ¾ mile (1.2 km) directly south of Silbury Hill. With all these small circles, there is no clear indication of their date of construction, or how they fitted in with the rest of the ceremonial landscape of Avebury. They almost certainly belong to the period when sarsen stones became a popular medium for the later Neolithic – early Bronze Age builders, between 2300 and 1800 BC.

Phasing, dating and construction of the ditch

There is much argument as to whether the circles at Avebury predate the great bank and ditch or vice versa. Some believe that it would have been too difficult to bring the stones across the causewayed entrances, and therefore the ditch must have been dug afterwards. However, evidence from other henge sites suggests that the construction of the bank and ditch enclosure was the primary function of the site, and therefore stone or wooden circles were of secondary importance, and would have been added after the ditch was dug. At present there are no radio-carbon dates associated with deposits from the Avebury circle, and we are therefore dependent on comparative data to indicate the sequence of events in the construction of the monument.

Beneath the bank at Avebury, a quantity of pottery was found scattered in the buried soil and in the lower levels of chalk and soil. The earlier Neolithic Windmill Hill ware was found in small quantities, showing that there had been activity in the immediate location of the circle from around the period 3200–2800 BC. Most of the pottery dated from the middle to later Neolithic period, and was represented by Peterborough types and associated Rinyo-Clacton styles, very similar to material from the later Neolithic occupation site on the Avenue. No Beaker pottery was found in the content of the bank, and we may conclude that the bank must date from the later Neolithic, and before the Beaker period in the final centuries of the third millennium BC. The material excavated from the bottom of the ditch was identical to the Windmill Hill and Peterborough pottery found under the bank, only it was more weathered and had probably been on the ground surface longer. The secondary fill of the ditch, probably derived from the weathering of the ditch sides after decades and centuries, contained sherds of Beaker pottery. This lack of Beaker material in the base layers does suggest that the ditch was dug before Beakers had appeared, and therefore must belong to the later Neolithic period, perhaps between 2600 and 2200 BC.

In most of the excavated stoneholes, scatters

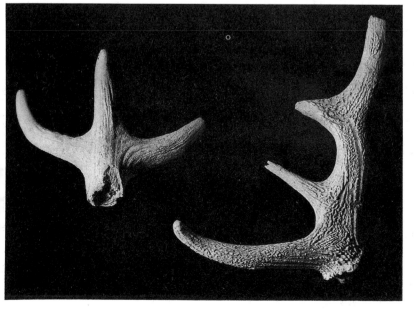

92 *Antler picks from the bottom of the henge ditch.*

of weathered Windmill Hill pottery was found, together with Beaker sherds, and this, with the associated evidence of the Beaker burials along the Avenue and in the circle, suggests that the bulk of the stones were erected in the Beaker period. This would agree well with the data from the Sanctuary, and from other henge sites, where the bulk of stone building seems to correspond with the final years of the Neolithic and the beginnings of the Bronze Age. Only a few outlying stones, such as the Ring stone, midway between the southern circle and the Portal stones, might date from an earlier phase, since some of these were packed with the lower chalk, found only at the base of the ditch, and thus appear to be contemporary with the ditch construction.

The ditch itself appears to have been excavated by gangs of workers, each with a given length to excavate. The result was an irregular width and depth along the whole length, with

93 *Plan of the terminal end of the ditch, east of the southern entrance, showing the burial of a human female dwarf together with other human bones, and deer antler pick and ox scapulae in situ, as left by the Neolithic excavators on completion of their work.*

sharp contrasts between one stretch and the next. Each gang probably excavated down, with a quarry-face at one end of the trench, and once they had achieved sufficient depth and width, the trench wall dividing it from the next was broken down, to join up with the main ditch.

The tools used were simple and effective. Wooden tools have not survived, but it is quite possible that wooden spades, digging sticks and the like were used. More effective, however, and capable of surviving the centuries to be excavated, were deer antler picks (**92**) and rakes, and ox scapula shovels. These were used to hack out lumps of chalk, which were then scraped into baskets or perhaps leather bags and slings. Somehow these heavy loads were then carried or winched up to the ground surface above, and then piled up to form the bank. It has been estimated that the excavation of the ditch took 156,000 man-hours, or three years' work for 100 men. This estimate may be too low, but we cannot know how efficient the Neolithic workers were. What is clear, however, is that the workforce was probably made up of both males and females, and that the average age of people working on the site was very low, quite possibly with young teenagers doing much of the work. The average age of the

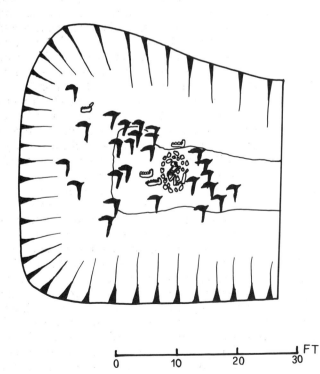

⊐ Human Jaw

Female Dwarf burial

Antler Pick

N

0   10   20   30 FT

population was very much younger than ours today, and if the elderly, very young, infirm, expectant and nursing mothers were excluded from the workforce, then those available to work would be the males, young adults and juveniles of the population.

The antler and scapular tools that were used to excavate the ditch were carefully deposited on the base of the ditch each side of the causewayed entrances, perhaps as religious offerings on the completion of the work. Gray found over 40 antlers alone in his 1908–22 excavations (**93**). Similar deposits of antlers were found at Windmill Hill, along the base of the ditches, and in Silbury Hill.

The function of the henge

When all the evidence about the henge is put together, considerable information is available about its construction, its vital statistics and its date. What is less clear, and not preserved in solid archaeological form, is its purpose. No amount of digging or speculating will provide much secure information on how the site was used, and we must rely to some extent on ethnographic parallels, where ceremonial and ritual events have been recorded in traditional societies, and on calculated guesses about what was both possible and likely in prehistoric society in Wessex.

It is usually accepted that Stonehenge in its later phases was designed as a simple calendar and astronomical observatory. Very simple sightings can be made observing the rising sun shining through the central trilithons of the inner horseshoe of stones on Midsummer Day. In the earlier phases of Stonehenge the Neolithic community were not apparently concerned with this, and the site was orientated rather differently. At Avebury, the irregular shape of the outer circle and the ditch, together with the off-centre inner circles, seem to have little relation to any calendrical or astronomical orientation. Only the Cove might have been used in that way, possibly for sighting the sun at midwinter. Stukeley, speculating in the 1720s, suggested that the northern inner circle was dedicated to the moon, and the southern to the sun, and accordingly named them the Lunar and Solar circles.

The role played by the circles at Avebury probably replaced that of Windmill Hill, as a central meeting place for special, ceremonial and ritual events. Festivals, perhaps marking the changing seasons, perhaps births and deaths may have been central themes. Several researchers have suggested that fertility was a central issue in later Neolithic society, and that the upright stones of the circles were used to worship the earth gods, and formed the arena within which sacrifices were offered to ensure good weather and harvests, and perhaps in order to ensure fertility amongst the population as well. As suggested earlier, the stones might have been intended to represent male and female, and could be seen as part of a fertility cult. However, no fragment of information has been found within Avebury that can confirm or deny these ideas, and it is all too possible that most material that formed part of the ceremonies would be of a type which deteriorated quickly. Grain, fruit and vegetables, and other agricultural offerings were probably eaten the same day they were offered. Animal sacrifices, although not the bones, would go in the same way.

The evidence for the burial of human remains is stronger, and several stones produced fragments of human burials at their bases. Human remains were also found in the bank and ditch, and some seven individuals were located in the small sections dug by Gray between 1908–1922 (see Chapter 9). All but two of these remains were either skulls, mandibles or long bones, very comparable to the material found in the ditches of Windmill Hill, and quite probably removed from the long barrows for special ritual purposes. They were similarly buried in the ditch with some ceremony, either together, or with grave-goods or burnt material. The most complete burial (**93**), in the terminal end of the ditch, was of a female dwarf, surrounded by small sarsen stones, and associated with a variety of deer antlers and animal bone which had also been carefully deposited there. She appears to have been a dedicatory burial placed in the ditch on its completion. It seems clear that human remains, perhaps of revered ancestors, continued to play a role in the rituals of Avebury. Other possibly symbolic items found include chalk balls and stone discs, but Avebury was kept very clean throughout its use, and almost nothing remains of any rubbish – animal bone, flint or pottery – that might have indicated what sort of activities were practised. The occupation site on the West Kennet Avenue may also have played an important role in the ceremonials, and many of its features are comparable to other non-habitation sites. Oolitic limestone, identical to that used in the West Kennet barrow, was found, and pits dug to bury the remains of feasts can be paralleled by those on the causewayed enclosures and under some long barrows. Likewise, the four pits behind the Obelisk in the southern circle at Avebury could be seen in relation to similar empty pits under long barrows, perhaps dug for special ritual purposes such as libations, and afterwards filled with clean soil.

The Obelisk has been interpreted as a phallic symbol, and therefore associated with fertility. The strange, squarish enclosure of small stones around it could be seen as a representation of a long barrow marked out on the ground, with the Obelisk, the fertility symbol, representing the human burials.

The evidence for the meaning of Avebury is thus very tentative. A monument dedicated to ceremonies for fertility, birth and death seems the most probable interpretation of what otherwise is a totally enigmatic monument. Without some very clear new evidence from the site, we can only make tentative guesses. We can imagine a gathering of people in late summer, massed from all the surrounding districts. The high banks all around would have acted as a stadium, and people perhaps crowded onto them to gain a better view of the ceremonies within the circle. Possibly only certain people were allowed inside – the chiefs, elders and wise men who conducted the ceremonies, young people undergoing special initiation rites, pregnant women wanting to make offerings to the fertility gods, farmers bringing offerings from their successful harvests – all entering through the great Portal stones, in view of the surrounding crowds. Chanting, special dances, drums and musical instruments would have accompanied the rituals (**colour plate 11**). Animals might have been slaughtered, and perhaps their blood, or perhaps mead or honey, was poured over particular stones, dedicated to gods with various powers. Harvest products could have been arranged around stones, to the chanted words of an elder; and natural signs, such as wind, sun, moon, stars and birds observed, in the hope of guaranteeing a propitious future harvest. Once the special ceremonies were complete, the real or symbolic barriers at the entrances might have been opened, letting all the watching crowds into the circles, for hours of dancing and revelry. At other seasons, different ceremonies might have brought the surrounding populations together again, perhaps for the sombre rituals of death, or to pay homage to a new moon, or a solstice.

9

The Henge: later history and excavation

The Avebury henge and its avenues remained in use in the early Bronze Age, but by the time the Wessex culture of the middle to later Bronze Age had become dominant in the area, Neolithic rituals appear to have been abandoned. Sites such as Windmill Hill were used for the location of splendid round barrows, and all along the crests of the downland overlooking the Avenue and Avebury, barrows were also constructed. The Ridgeway path also became a focus of these burials, and as fig. **5** shows, the Avebury area was spotted with the evidence of Bronze Age funerary constructions. There seems little doubt that the once important Neolithic sites ceased to be used in the traditional ceremonial manner, but nevertheless, the sites apparently still retained a special significance. No disturbance took place and the stones remained intact. Some probably fell over, and the area became overgrown and neglected.

By the Iron Age, attention had moved away from the Avebury area to the higher downland, where fortified hillforts were being built by rival tribes, each defending their territories. The steep scarps above the Vale of Pewsey and along the northern edge of the downs at Uffington and above Swindon became hilltop refuges, (see **6**) and there appears to have been no activity at Avebury. In the Roman period, Avebury was hardly noticed, and although there was Roman settlement in the area, no one disturbed the stones of the monuments. Some Roman pottery in the upper layers of the ditch suggests that people may have visited the henge either out of curiosity or simply to dump rubbish. A major Roman road connecting Bath with Mildenhall, whose line is now followed by

94 *Aerial view of Avebury looking east, showing the church, the manor on the site of the Benedictine priory on the left, and the location of the Saxon-medieval and modern village on the right.*

the A4, passed within one mile of the site, and diverted around the edge of Silbury Hill.

In the Saxon period, the high bank and ditch offered a secure and semi-defended location for settlement, and a Saxon or perhaps native Celtic community used the site as the focus for a stronghold of some type. Most of the settlement was just outside the western banks of the henge, and long houses with sunken floors covered the area. This settlement probably existed from the

119

sixth to the ninth century AD, and by the eleventh century a thriving village was in existence. The 'dyke of the Britons', 'Weala-dic' or 'Waledich', as it was known, expanded into the circle sometime after the eleventh century.

Medieval Avebury

The origins of the village of Avebury are not well recorded, and the archaeology that survives in the ground, together with the fabric of the church, provides most of the information available today. It is likely that the stones,

95 *Saxon and medieval field systems to the west of Avebury, near the site of the Saxon village.*

96 *The skull and long bones of the medieval barber-surgeon found under a partially-fallen buried stone in the south west sector of Avebury in 1938.*

which were probably all still visible in the tenth century AD, even if some had fallen down, were the focus of pagan cults and beliefs. Names associated with devil worship abounded: the Cove in the north circle was known as the Devil's Brandirons, the Beckhampton long-stones as the Devil's Quoits, the Portal stones as the Devil's Chair, and the megalithic chamber tomb at Clatford as the Devil's Den – all of them names which have come down to the present day. Christianity was making a renewed effort in the early medieval period to consolidate its position in English society: churches and monasteries were being founded and missionaries were active. At Avebury, the threat of ancient pagan cults to orthodox religion was all too clear, with the inexplicable stones of vast size dominating the landscape. The Saxons built the first church in the ninth or tenth century AD, and this was followed by the foundation of a small Benedictine priory on the site of what is now Avebury Manor in 1114, and of an oratory in 1180. The church was further enlarged in the later twelfth century, and its fine carved font added. Significantly, the church was sited immediately outside the banks of the henge, and north of the Saxon village. The divine presence of the church could be thus seen to be challenging the ancient henge; and the local clerics and monks began a campaign which resulted in the destruction of much of ancient Avebury.

By the later twelfth and early thirteenth centuries, the campaign to rid the residents of Avebury of their pagan inspiration, the standing stones, had begun in earnest, and it seems that groups of people were organized into workparties, and directed to a stone, armed with iron spades, tools and crowbars. They then proceeded to dig a deep pit beside the standing stone, and then, once it was deep enough, toppled the stone over, and buried it completely under the ground. Once the grass had grown back, there was little hint of where the stone had once stood. The interior of Avebury was used for gardens and for the dumping of household rubbish, and this material found its way into the stone pits, along with the stones, giving a clear date when the stones were buried. Not all the stones were buried, but many, such as the Obelisk were toppled over.

The best evidence for the stone burying comes from one particular tragedy. In the south-west sector of Avebury, stone 9 was being buried in a partially finished pit, when it fell over unexpectedly, crushing one of the work-force, a man, who died immediately from a broken pelvis and neck (**96**). No attempt was made to extract his body, and instead it was buried with the stone. In the man's leather purse was a pair of scissors, an iron probe and three silver coins, two being pennies of Edward I, and the third a French sterling of Toul (Normandy). The coins as a group were dated to some time after 1310, and probably the accident happened between 1320 and 1325. The presence of the tools is interesting, since the scissors and probe might well be associated with an itinerant worker, who had been press-ganged into some manual work by the church during a visit to Avebury. He may have been a barber-surgeon, who went from village to village, cutting hair and nails, pulling teeth and lancing abscesses and the like.

Many stones had disappeared or were half-buried in the grass by the time the Reformation brought about the closure and destruction of the priory and the new manor had been founded on the same spot. The Catholic parishioners, knowing that the church was to be despoiled, quickly acted to save one of their treasures, the rood screen, before the church authorities forced them to destroy it. The screen was taken down, turned to the chancel wall, and plastered over, where it remained undiscovered until the nineteenth century. The surviving upper parts have now been put back in place, with a nine-teenth-century restoration of the lower portion, and the original colours still survive intact. It is one of the best examples of its type surviving.

The manor was built in the Tudor style, and added to through the following century with splendid early sixteenth-century features such as its windows and west front. Much of the stone used in its construction came from the demolished priory, and also from the Megalithic stones in the circle. It was during the later seventeenth century that the systematic destruction of the standing stones began in order to provide building stone for a growing industry of house-building in Avebury. Until that period, most buildings in Avebury had been timber-framed wattle and daub structures, but changing styles and an improving standard of living demanded more solidly-built houses. Local builders devised a method of breaking the great stones into small manageable fragments. A pit was dug at the base of the stone, and then filled with straw which was set alight until the stone became hot. Then cold water was poured over one part of the stone, followed by a sharp tap from a sledgehammer, and the stone would then fall into fragments. Inevitably, the fracturing of the stone also resulted in masses of tiny, useless fragments, which were left in the burning pit, together with clay pipes and broken tools. The destruction continued until about 1825, and builders were sufficiently desperate for stone, that they actually excavated some of those buried in the medieval period, and destroyed these as well. By 1812, a survey by Crocker showed that only 35 or 36 stones remained visible in the circle, and 20 in the Avenue.

Nineteenth-century antiquarians and their discoveries

After Aubrey and Stukeley (see pp. 21–6), the next antiquarians to record Avebury were Sir Richard Colt Hoare and his assistant, William Cunnington, who had excavated barrows all over Salisbury Plain. They visited the site in 1812, during their tour of north Wiltshire, for the preparation of Hoare's book *Ancient Wiltshire*, published in 1821. Their draughtsman, P. Crocker, made a survey of the site, showing that 12 more circle stones had vanished since Stukeley's plans were made in the 1720s. Other researchers recorded more stones as they were removed, and they sometimes recorded what

became of them. One of these, Joseph Hunter was told in 1829 that one large stone had been used to make a wall beside the road through Avebury, and that the ground around the Cove had been dug to see if sacrifices had been performed there. Most writing about Avebury was of a more speculative nature, and in 1867 the famous archaeologist, James Fergusson author of *Rude Stone Monuments*, pronounced that Avebury was the great burial ground of Arthur's warrors. Others suggested it was a calendar, an astronomical observatory, and a temple, following the lead given by Stukeley. Various antiquarians dug holes in the circle, in an attempt to find out the date or purpose of the site. They mostly found burning holes, pits, and broken sarsen stone, but William Cunnington and A. C. Smith did manage to locate two buried stones in the south-west sector in 1865. They also dug into the banks of the site, but no record remains of what they found. Smith followed this work up with more probing, and discovered that there were at least 15 buried stones in the eastern half of the outer circle in 1881. This has still not been explored, and the stones may be presumed to be there still.

During 1872 there were plans to build more new houses within the henge, and Sir John Lubbock, an archaeologist and member of Parliament, became very active in an attempt to save the site. He managed to buy part of

97 *The cove photographed with Mrs Gray and her son in 1908 when Harold St George Gray first began work at Avebury.*

98 *Gray's excavations in the south-west sector of Avebury between 1908 and 1914. Only two stones are visible in the sector.*

it and eventually pushed through a Bill in Parliament to protect ancient monuments, the first Ancient Monuments Act of 1882, which scheduled protected sites for the first time. Until then, there had been no statutory listing of historical sites. Public opinion was very opposed to legislation, regarding it as an infringement of the rights of ownership. Avebury was now however, a protected site and no more destruction could legally take place.

Another owner of the site, Sir Henry Meux, became interested in the monument, and dug a trench into the bank in 1894, near the south-east entrance, leaving a scar that is visible today. He found the buried ground surface beneath the bank, and also a number of flints and pieces of pottery.

Harold St George Gray and the excavation of the henge

It was clear to concerned bodies of archaeologists that further uncontrolled digging in Avebury and other stone circles was unlikely to achieve useful results, and a project was set up by the British Association for the Advancement of Science to explore the 'Age of the Stone Circles'. The eminent archaeologist Harold St George Gray was made the director, and began with excavations at Arbor Low in Derbyshire in 1902. These were followed by investigations at Stanton Drew circles in Somerset, and then in 1908 Gray came to Avebury, for his largest series of excavations for the Association's project.

99 *Gray's deep section through the great ditch at Avebury in 1922, showing the depth of deposit, with his workmen lined up.*

Five seasons of work over the period 1908–1922 were organized by Gray, and numerous cuttings were made into the ditch (**98,99**), showing its enormous depth, and the stratigraphic nature of the deposits. Gray was a meticulous excavator, having been trained by the great General Pitt-Rivers, on sites throughout Wessex. His survey of Avebury was faultless, and his notebooks, which still survive, show the detail which he recorded in the excavation trenches.

Gray discovered for the first time that Avebury was a Neolithic monument. He unearthed flint tools, pottery fragments, human and animal bone, and the tools from the original ditch excavation. These were deer antler picks and rakes (**92**), and ox scapulae, which had been

100 *The Avebury bank and ditch as Keiller found it in 1936, covered in trees, scrub and rubbish.*

carefully laid at the base of the completed ditch (**93**). Gray noticed all these details, and also the composition of each layer of soil and chalk in the ditch. He collected samples of snails, bone and stone in an attempt to make a full scientific analysis of the ditch contents.

The project itself did not progress without hitches. In particular, Gray was keen to excavate on the east side of the southern causewayed entrance, knowing it had not been disturbed, but was only able to do this in 1914, once the unwilling tenant had been persuaded. It was at this terminal end of the ditch that the picks, scapulae and burial of a female dwarf came to light. He was also always short of funds, and each year had to present an appeal to the British Association and its subscribers for more funding in the following season. Remarkably small sums of money by modern standards were required, and £40 given for the 1914 excavation was considered quite adequate. The war years of 1914–18 also prevented much work being done after 1914, and the project finally came to an end in 1922.

Gray does not appear to have been interested

in the standing stones, and little of his research was directed towards them. He did, however, take some photographs of the site which preserve details of the almost stoneless and rather derelict place that Avebury had become in the early twentieth century (**98**).

Keiller and the reconstruction of the circle

Avebury remained in a variety of ownerships until Alexander Keiller finally bought the whole site in 1934. It was only then that the site was tidied up and excavated. When Keiller took over Avebury, it was 'the national archaeological disgrace of Britain' being encumbered with pigsties, a garage with derelict pumps, a windmill, shabby cottages, rubbish everywhere and all overgrown and obscured beneath trees and scrub (**100, 101**).

Keiller began excavation work on the Avenue, and began the task of clearing up Avebury. The garage and its mess was removed and a new garage built north of the circle. Corrugated iron sheds, latrines and pigsties were swept away, and in order to remove the trees and their roots, a New Zealand explosives expert was brought in to set charges around the felled trunks. This method of tree removal proved to be successful, and there was little disturbance to the bank of the henge. Once the Avenue excavations were complete in 1935, work began in earnest on the circle in 1936, with a survey and clearance of rubbish. Its restoration had become almost an obsession for

101 *The interior of the great henge at Avebury in 1936 was cluttered with pigsties, sheds and old agricultural rubbish.*

102 *Such was the accumulation of rubbish and soil in the Avebury henge that Keiller brought in modern excavation equipment to remove the worse of it. Here work takes place in the south-east sector in 1939.*

Keiller, and he poured all his resources into the project.

In 1937, the first season of work began in the north-west sector of the circle. Four stones were still standing and another four could be identified on the ground. This sector had been the worst affected by the tree cover, and much of the surface soil was rough and root-filled and required modern earth-moving equipment to help with the task of clearance (**102**). Nevertheless, excavations successfully revealed a further eight buried stones, and they were re-set in their original setting in the same way as the stones in the Avenue. Some stones had been badly damaged by early attempts to crack them into building stones, and after careful piecing together, these were pinned with steel rods. One stone near the north causewayed entrance was

never quite completed, and still has odd stone lumps attached, awaiting full restoration.

The following year, work concentrated on the south-west sector where just one stone remained standing and three more were just visible. This involved the removal of the blacksmith's shop which had stood opposite the manor farm house. Beneath this was found the remains of a much-broken stone that had been incorporated into the foundations. The great ditch, even since Gray's excavations, had become choked with village refuse, and Keiller had this cleared and removed, down to the level of natural silting. Excavation concentrated only on the area where the outer stone circle was known to stand, and all the top soil was removed to expose the natural chalk beneath. Once this was cleaned, any holes dug through for stoneholes or for eighteenth-century burning pits could be clearly identified. Packing material of chalk and soil concealed buried stones which were found often several feet below the ground surface. A total of seven buried stones were restored to join the four that were still visible. Keiller, having experimented

103 *Large winches and pulleys and massive scaffolding of timber were used to hoist fallen and buried stones into their original positions. Here, a stone is raised in the south-west sector in 1939.*

with the traditional methods of raising stones on the Avenue, was content to have more modern and efficient equipment to raise the fallen and buried stones, and massive winches and pulleys were used (**103**).

It was in the south-west sector that the best dating evidence for the original destruction of the circle came to light, with the discovery of the Barber-Surgeon stone (see p.121). Medieval pottery had been found in great quantities in many of the stone holes and in the top soil of the circle, but the presence of the skeleton together with his dated coins provided the best information. Other finds in the eighteenth-century burning pits included hammers, crowbars and straw rakes that had been used to pull the stones down for burning.

1939 was the final season of excavation and restoration, and work continued through the summer until war was declared. Excavation concentrated not on the outer stones, but instead on the internal setting of the southeast sector's southern circle. Knowing that the Obelisk recorded by Stukeley had been located there, Keiller concentrated on the remaining stones of the southern circle. Two remained standing and three were visible. The site of the Obelisk was found, and behind it the four curious pits. More unexpected was the setting of smaller stones around the Obelisk: rough sarsens, aligned in what appeared to be a rectangular enclosure, known as the 'Z' feature. Eight stones were found, and the stone holes for six more. In the outer circle, only stone holes were identified, all the remaining stones having been destroyed in the eighteenth century. Had war not broken out, Keiller certainly planned to continue his work on the southern circle, and to find the complete shape of the 'Z' feature. He had not intended to investigate more stones in the outer circle until archaeological methods had improved. As it is, nothing more except some small trial holes in the northeast sector has been done at Avebury since Keiller's work. Many stones remain under ground, known from probing work in the last

104 *Large areas of top soil were stripped to expose the buried stones beneath. Here the alignment of stones in the southern circle lies ready for further investigation in 1939.*

105 *The original site of the long-destroyed Obelisk in the southern circle was marked by a specially-designed plinth in 1939.*

century, and perhaps one day will also be un-covered in a further programme of restoration.

In the same way that Windmill Hill had been a pioneering excavation, so too was the work at Avebury. A small team of skilled archaeologists, most of whom had already worked on the Avenue excavations, continued to work at Ave-bury, as part of the research team of Keiller's Morven Institute of Archaeological Research which was based in the coach house of the manor house. The methods of survey and record-ing begun on Windmill Hill, and continued on the Avenue, were further refined. Photography played an important role in the process, and every stone hole, stone or feature was fully recorded. Keiller employed local workmen, supervised by his site assistant, Willie Young, and took the photographs and did much of

the technical survey work himself. Young had worked with Keiller since the first season at Windmill Hill, and was taken on permanently as the curator of the coach-house museum. Whilst work was in progress over the summers of 1937 to 1939, the Avebury henge was open to visitors, who were guided by signs around the trenches. Stones were being excavated, and hoisted back into their original positions, amid much publicity, and public applause. The same sentiments were not shared by the locals, some of whom vigorously protested that the stones were being discriminately dragged from the ground, and the site desecrated for those who preferred it romantic, anonymous, and tree-covered.

Keiller was enthusiastic about the public presentation of the fresh archaeology emerging from the ground, providing on site information, and opening his private museum with all the Windmill Hill material on show in the coach house to any interested visitor. Such an

106 *The original didactic display of Windmill Hill pottery in Keiller's private museum at Ave-bury.*

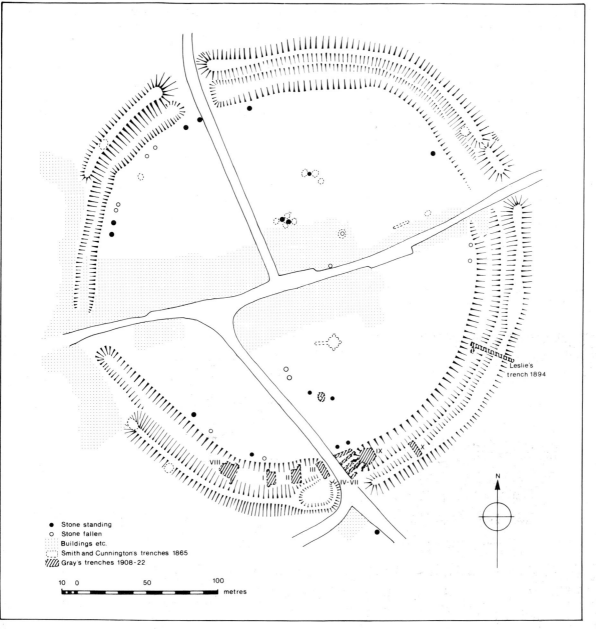

107 *Plan of Avebury before Keiller began work on the henge in 1936.*

approach was quite a rare thing in the 1930s, but one that has since become a major part of modern archaeology. Keiller was determined to provide access and archaeological information for the public, and it was in this spirit that he began to investigate ways of ensuring that his work at Avebury would continue to be part of the national heritage.

Avebury today

Once Keiller had completed the 1939 season of work at Avebury, he began to promote the idea of presenting Avebury to the nation. The National Trust was the obvious organization to take charge of it at the time, but required a substantial endowment in order to take the site on for perpetuity. A public subscription was organized, and within a few months the necessary sum was raised. The area around Avebury was designated a conservation zone, and farm-

131

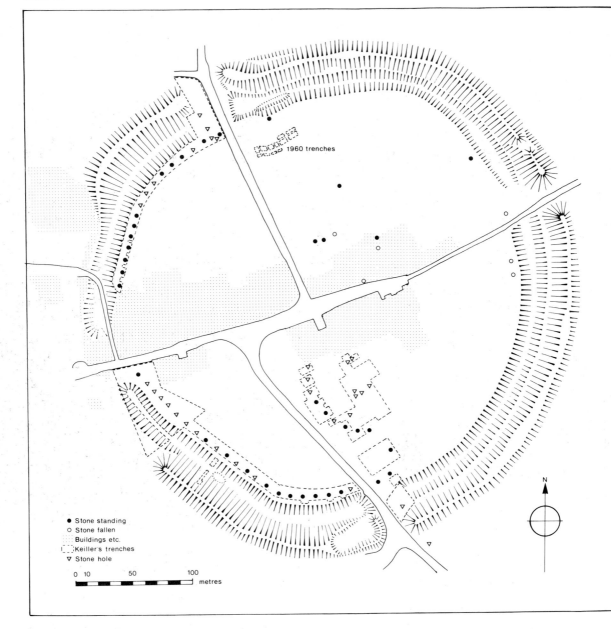

1960 trenches

● Stone standing
○ Stone fallen
⬚ Buildings etc.
⬚ Keiller's trenches
▽ Stone hole

0 10   50   100
⊢━━━━━━━━━━━━━━━┙ metres

N

108 *Plan of Avebury after three seasons of excavation and restoration at Avebury in 1939.*

land together with most of the cottages within the Avebury henge, were included in the estate which was finally handed over to the National Trust during the war. The site also became a Guardianship Site under the then Office of Works, (now English Heritage), and has been jointly managed by the two bodies ever since.

For some years, the policy begun by Keiller

of pulling down redundant cottages and barns within the circle, was continued, and the stone building beside the Cove (see **97, 101**) was removed, as were cottages opposite the Red Lion Inn at the crossroads. Eventually however, such a policy was regarded as vandalism since the buildings are also an integral part of the history of Avebury, and their presence added both scale and a modern purpose to the ancient site.

Now Avebury is a thriving community of

109 *Avebury restored, soon after the newly-cleaned stones had been re-erected and the whole area was returfed and landscaped in 1939.*

local residents, commuters and custodians. Since 1979 the full potential of Avebury as one of the primary ancient sites of Britain has been realized, and along with this have come the trappings of modern tourism, (cafes, postcards, guided tours, coaches, large car parks), and commercial enterprises hover hopefully seeing the quarter of a million visitors a year as a veritable honeypot. It would be sad if the once rural and mysterious peace of Avebury were to be shattered by excessive tourist facilities, and only careful controls will prevent it.

Regardless of the popular threats to Avebury as a village and tourist centre, the site has gained much importance through being classified as one of the World Heritage Sites. This designation includes all the principal monuments described in this book as part of the Avebury landscape. Few other prehistoric sites in Europe have been so classified, and this status may yet help to protect this vulnerable ancient place for the future.

Appendix

Suggested tour of the Avebury sites

Avebury, located 10 miles south of Swindon and 5 miles west of Marlborough is easily accessible by car from the M4 and the A4. Occasional public buses run from Swindon through Avebury, and some coach tour companies include Avebury. For the walker, Avebury, located only 1 mile (1.5 km) west of the Ridgeway long distance footpath, is a delightful beginning or end to the footpath.

Ordnance Survey Maps

No. 173 (Swindon and Devizes) at 1:50 000 provides cover of the whole Avebury area and shows the principal sites and footpaths. More detailed maps at 1:25 000 are SU 16 (The Marlborough Downs), SU 17 (Marlborough), SU 06 (Devizes) and SU 07 (Lynham). Grid references given for the various sites below refer to these maps.

Visitor facilities

Avebury forms the focus for most visitors, having both year-round and seasonal facilities. Car parking is available south of Avebury circle, with access from the A4316. Footpaths lead to Avebury (219 yds/200 m) and south to Silbury.

In Avebury, information is available from the English Heritage Alexander Keiller Museum and shop, and from the Great Barn Museum of Wiltshire Folk Life, which is also the agent for the English Tourist Board. The National Trust Shop opposite the Great Barn (seasonally open) sells books and gifts, and Stones Restaurant provides meals and snacks throughout the day. There is a Post Office and other gift and antique shops within the village. Bed and breakfast accommodation is available, and can be booked through the Great Barn Museum.

The Alexander Keiller Museum is open throughout the year with displays of archaeological artefacts excavated at Avebury and Windmill Hill. Summer hours are from 9 am to 6 pm; winter (October to March) 9 am to 4 pm; and it is closed on December 24, 25, 26 and January 1. Books and postcards on the archaeological sites are available.

Tour

Each of the sites can be visited separately, and cars can be parked within about 219 yds (200 m) of each of them. However, all the sites can be reached easily in one day on foot, via public footpaths, and cars can be left in the main car park at Avebury.

Avebury (GR 103700)

To appreciate the scale of Avebury, a walk around the perimeter of the circle is recommended. Leaving the main car park, follow the footpath to Avebury High Street, and enter the south-west quadrant. Information panels provide orientation in each sector. The south-west sector, excavated in 1938, revealed several buried stones, including that of the barber-surgeon. All the stones found were re-set, and missing stones marked with concrete plinths. Following the stones round, cross the road into the south-east sector where excavations took place on the inner circle in 1939. The Obelisk is marked by a large concrete plinth and is surrounded by the smaller stones of the 'Z' feature setting. Several larger stones of the inner southern circle were excavated and set upright and give a clear impression of the scale and grandeur of the circle. Ridges of old fields can be identified in the quadrant. Proceeding towards the southern causewayed entrance (used by the modern road), climb the bank and follow it round to the east causewayed entrance. Remnants of the berm or flat area between the bank and ditch edge can be made out in places. The Ridgeway can be seen clearly on the eastern horizon, with numerous round barrows forming humps under clumps of trees.

Crossing Green Street, which leads up to the Ridgeway, enter the north-east sector. Here little excavation has been undertaken, and few stones are visible. The main interest in the quadrant is the Cove, with its two remaining stones. Cross the Swindon Road into the north-west quadrant and follow the stones around the edge of the circle. Keiller began his excavations in this sector in 1937, and many of the standing stones visible today have been pieced together. Exit behind the Great Barn and proceed either to the Alexander Keiller Museum and Barn complex, manor and church, or on past these on foot to Windmill Hill.

Windmill Hill (GR 086715) can be reached by car from the A4361, taking the turning west of Avebury to Avebury Trusloe (signed from the road) and following Ancient Monument signs north, past cottages and farms for about half a mile (700 m) uphill to Windmill Hill. Parking is in an unofficial layby where the tarmac ends, about 219 yds (200 m) short of the site. It is not advisable to drive further than the tarmac! From there proceed on foot up the track to the pedestrian gate. Enter the site, and aim towards the north-east, keeping the Bronze Age barrows on your right. After about 55 yds (50 m) you will begin to see the low ridges of the surviving banks of the causewayed enclosures. These are best preserved on the eastern flanks of the hill, where parts of the formerly excavated ditch can also be distinguished. The barrow group is worth examining, since the ditches around each individual barrow are well-defined.

By foot from Avebury, leave by the footpath on the west side of the churchyard, and proceed towards Avebury Trusloe, taking the right fork where the path divides and passing Trusloe Manor. Continue along the path, which merges into a track and then road, until reaching a junction, where you take the right-hand fork. This is the road to Windmill Hill, which ascends as described above. Other paths (see OS maps) lead back to Avebury via Winterbourne Monkton, and east to the A4361.

The Long Stones of the Beckhampton Avenue can be seen west of Avebury Trusloe although there is no official access, and can be reached by the lane (South Street) that runs parallel to the A4361 (first turning left after

turning in towards Avebury Trusloe). The site of South Street long barrow is beside the lane but is no longer visible.

The West Kennet Avenue extends south from Avebury, and can be visited from the stone circle, leaving from the south causewayed entrance. Only the northern third of the Avenue is accessible, but many stones have been restored and give an excellent impression of the original ceremonial route. There is a small layby at the southern end of the avenue for access to the stones.

Silbury Hill is located beside the A4 (GR 100686) and has a small car park for the use of visitors. There is no access to the hill itself, since the area is protected as a Site of Special Scientific Interest, preserving fragile and rare plant species. However, there is an excellent viewing area. From Avebury, walkers can follow the footpath that leaves from opposite the main Avebury car park, and walk the $\frac{3}{4}$ mile (1 km) beside the stream, south to Silbury.

The West Kennet long barrow is situated a short distance east of Silbury Hill, on the south side of the A4, and has a small layby at the footpath leading to the site (GR 105677). Walkers can follow the A4 the 350 yards (300 m) to continue their tour. A fairly rugged quarter-mile (400 m) footpath is the only access to the barrow. Once you reach the barrow, access can be gained to the interior of the chambers and passage at any time, and excellent views of Silbury, East Kennet barrow and the Sanctuary can be seen. Walkers can proceed east along the River Kennett, following the footpath to West Kennet Village, from there across the river to the A4, and then up the lane to Avebury following the West Kennet Avenue.

The Sanctuary on Overton Hill (GR 118679) is beside the A4, and opposite a cafe. There is a layby and ample parking space. The Sanctuary is now marked out by concrete markers, showing the different phases of the site. From the site, there are excellent views in all directions and also of the fine round barrows beside the Ridgeway path. Walkers can follow the Ridgeway north, until the path branches left to Avebury, and can complete their circuit by entering Avebury by Green Street.

Other sites worth visiting are Knap Hill, the Devil's Den at Clatford, and the natural scatters of sarsen stones at Piggledene and Fyfield.

Further reading

1 Avebury: the survival of an ancient landscape

Anderson, J.R.L., and Godwin, Fay (1975), *The oldest road: the exploration of the Ridgeway*, Wildwood House, London.

Atkinson, R.J.C. (1959), *Stonehenge and Avebury*, HMSO, London.

Barratt, J.C., and Bradley, R. (1980) (eds.), *Settlement and society in the later British Bronze Age*, British Archaeological Reports 83, Oxford.

Bradley, R. (1984), *The social foundations of prehistoric Britain: themes and variations in the archaeology of power*, Longman, London.

Burgess, C. (1980), *The age of Stonehenge*, J.M. Dent and Sons Ltd., London.

Darville, T. (1987), *Prehistoric Britain*, Batsford, London.

Harding, D.W. (1976) (ed.), *Hillforts – later prehistoric earthworks in Britain and Ireland*, Academic Press, London.

Jennett, S. (1980), *The Ridgeway Path*, Long-distance Footpath Guide No. 6, HMSO, London.

Piggott, S. (1938), 'The early bronze age in Wessex', *Proceedings of the Prehistoric Society* 4, 52–106.

Pitts, M. (1985), *Footprints through Avebury*, Stones Publications, Avebury.

Smith, I.F. (1974), 'The Neolithic' in Renfrew, A.C. (ed.), *British Prehistory: a new outline*.

Vatcher, F. (1979), *The Avebury Monuments*, HMSO, London.

Whittle, A.W.R. (1985), *Neolithic Europe: a survey*, Cambridge University Press, Cambridge.

2 The environment of Neolithic Avebury

Barron, R.S. (1976), *The Geology of Wiltshire: a field guide*, Moonraker Press, Bradford-upon-Avon.

Birks, H.J.B., Deacon, J., and Pegler, S. (1975), 'Pollen maps for the British Isles 5000 years ago', *Proceedings of the Royal Society of London* (B) 189, 87–105.

Burgess, C., and Miket, R. (1976) (eds.), 'Settlement and economy in the third millennium BC', *British Archaeological Reports* 33, Oxford.

Clarke, D.L. (1976), 'Mesolithic Europe: the economic basis' in Sieveking, G. De. G., Longworth, I.H., and Wilson, K.E. (eds.), *Problems in economic and social archaeology*, 449–81, Duckworth, London.

Dennell, R.W. (1976), 'Prehistoric crop cultivation in southern England', *Antiquaries Journal* 56, 11–23.

Evans, J.G. (1971), 'Habitat changes on the calcareous soils of Britain' in Simpson, D.D.A. (ed.), *Economy and settlement in Neolithic and early Bronze Age Britain and Europe*, Leicester University Press, Leicester.

Evans, J.G. (1975), *The environment of early man in the British Isles*, Paul Elek, London.

Evans, J.G. (1978), *An introduction to environmental archaeology*, Paul Elek, London.

Fowler, P.J. (1971), 'Early prehistoric agriculture in western Europe: some archaeological evidence' in Simpson, D.D.A. (ed.), *Economy and settlement in Neolithic and early Bronze Age Britain and Europe*, Leicester University Press, Leicester.

Fowler, P.J. (1983), *The farming of prehistoric Britain*, Cambridge University Press, Cambridge.

Jones, D.K.C. (1981), *The Geomorphology of the British Isles: South-east and southern England*, Methuen, London.

Mercer, R. (1981) (ed.), *Farming practice in British prehistory*, Edinburgh University Press, Edinburgh.

Renfrew, C. (1973) *Before Civilisation – the*

radio-carbon revolution and prehistoric Europe, Penguin Books, Harmondsworth.

Smith, R.W. (1984), 'The ecology of Neolithic farming systems as exemplified by the Avebury region of Wiltshire', *Proceedings of the Prehistoric Society* 50, 99–120.

3 Avebury and its monuments

Ashbee, P. (1984), *The earthen long barrow in Britain: an introduction to the study of funerary practice and culture of the Neolithic people of the III millennium BC,* (2nd ed.) Geo Books, Norwich.

Barker, G.W.W., and Webley, D. (1978), 'Causewayed camps and early Neolithic economies in central southern England', *Proceedings of the Prehistoric Society* 44, 161–86.

Bradley, R. (1984), *The social foundations of prehistoric Europe: themes and variations in the archaeology of power*, chapters 1–4. Longman, London.

Bradley, R., and Gardiner, J. (eds.) (1984), 'Neolithic Studies: a review of some current research', *British Archaeological Reports* 133, Oxford.

Burl, A. (1979), *Prehistoric Avebury*, Yale University Press, New Haven and London.

Fleming, A. (1973), 'Tombs for the Living', *Man* 8, 177–93.

Piggott, S. (1963), 'The West Kennet Long Barrow: excavations 1955–6' *Ministry of Works Archaeological Reports* No. 4, HMSO, London.

Sahlins, M.D. (1968), *Tribesmen*, Prentice Hall, New Jersey.

Shanks, M. and Tilley, C. (1982), 'Ideology, symbolic power and ritual communication: a reinterpretation of Neolithic mortuary practices' in Hodder, I. (ed.), *Symbolic and Structural Archaeology,* 129–54, Cambridge University Press.

Smith, I.F. (1965), *Windmill Hill and Avebury: excavations by Alexander Keiller 1925–39*, Clarendon Press, Oxford.

Whittle, A.W.R. (1981), 'Late Neolithic Society in Britain: a realignment' in Ruggles, C., and Whittle, A.W.R. (eds.), 'Astronomy and Society during the period 4000–150 BC', *British Archaeological Reports* 88, 297–342.

4 Windmill Hill

Cunnington, M.E. (1912), 'Knap Hill camp, Wiltshire', *Wiltshire Archaeological Magazine* 37, 42–65.

Dixon, P. (1972), *Crickley Hill: fourth report*, Cheltenham.

Liddell, D. (1930), 'Report on the excavations at Hembury Fort, Devon', *Proceedings of the Devon Archaeological Exploration Society* I (2), 39–63.

Liddell, D. (1931), 'Report of the excavations at Hembury Fort, Devon, (second season 1931)', *Proceedings of the Devon Archaeological Exploration Society* I (3), 90–120.

Liddell, D. (1932), 'Report on the excavations at Hembury Fort, Devon (third season)', *Proceedings of the Devon Archaeological Exploration Society* I (4), 162–90.

Liddell, D. (1935), 'Report on the excavations at Hembury Fort, Devon, (fourth and fifth seasons, 1934–1935)', *Proceedings of the Devon Archaeological Exploration Society* II (3), 135-75.

Mercer, R. (1980), *Hambledon Hill: a Neolithic landscape*, Edinburgh University Press: Edinburgh.

Palmer, R. (1976), 'Interrupted ditch enclosures in Britain: the use of aerial photography for comparative studies', *Proceedings of the Prehistoric Society* 47, 161–186.

Piggott, S. (1952), 'The Neolithic camp on Whitesheet Hill, Kilmington, *Wiltshire Archaeological Magazine* 56, 404–10.

Piggott, S. (1954), *Neolithic cultures of the British Isles*, Cambridge University Press, Cambridge.

Smith, I.F. (1965), *Windmill Hill and Avebury: excavations by Alexander Keiller 1925–39*, Clarendon Press, Oxford.

Smith, I.F. (1966), 'Windmill Hill and its implications', *Palaeohistoria* 12, 469–81.

Smith, I.F. (1971), 'Causewayed enclosures' in D.D.A. Simpson (ed.), *Economy and settlement in Neolithic and early Bronze Age Britain and Europe*, 89–112. Leicester University Press, Leicester.

Thomas, N. (1964), 'The Neolithic causewayed camp at Robin Hood's Ball, Shrewton', *Wiltshire Archaeological Magazine* 59, 1–27.

Whittle, A.W.R. (1977), 'Earlier Neolithic enclosures in north-west Europe'. *Proceedings of the Prehistoric Society* 43, 329–48.

5 The long barrows

Ashbee, P. (1966), 'The Fussell's Lodge long barrow excavations, 1957', *Archaeologia* 100, 1–80.

Ashbee, P. (1984), *The earthen Long Barrow in Britain*, (2nd ed.) Geo Books, Norwich.

Ashbee, P., and Smith, I.F. (1966), 'The date of the Windmill Hill long barrow', *Antiquity* 40, 299.

Ashbee, P., Smith, I.F., and Evans, J.G. (1979), 'Excavation of three long barrows near Avebury, Wiltshire', *Proceedings of the Pehistoric Society* 45, 207–300.

Atkinson, R.J.C. (1965), 'Wayland's Smith, Berkshire', *Antiquity* 39, 126–33.

Barker, C.T. (1984), 'The long mounds of the Avebury Region', *Wiltshire Archaeological Magazine* 79, 7–38.

Benson, D., and Clegg, I. (1978), 'Cotswold Burial Rites', *Man* 13, 134–6.

Corcoran, J.X.W.P. (1969), 'The Severn-Cotswold group' in Powell, T.G.E. *et al* (eds.), *Megalithic enquiries in the west of Britain*, 13–106, 273–95, Liverpool University Press, Liverpool.

Corcoran, J.X.W.P. (1972), 'Multi-period construction and the origins of the chambered long cairn in western Britain and Ireland' in Lynch, F.M., and Burgess, C. (eds.), *Prehistoric man in Wales and the West*, 31–64, Adams and Dart, Bath.

Darvill, T.C. (1982), *The megalithic chambered tombs of the Cotswold-Severn region*, Vorda, Highworth.

Piggott, S. (1963), 'The West Kennet Long Barrow: excavations 1955–6', *Ministry of Works Archaeological Reports* No. 4, HMSO, London.

Piggott, S. (1967), 'Unchambered long barrows in Neolithic Britain', *Palaeohistoria* 12, 381–93.

Piggott, S. (1973), 'Problems in the interpretation of chambered tombs', in Daniel, G.E., and Kjaerum, P. (eds.), *Megalithic graves and ritual*, 9–15, Jutland Archaeological Society, Copenhagen.

Selkirk, A. (1971), 'Ascott-under-Wychwood', *Current Archaeology* 24, 7–10.

Thurnham, J. (1860), 'Examination of a chambered long barrow at West Kennet, Wiltshire', *Archaeologia* 38, 405–21.

Whittle, A.W.R., and Thomas, J. (1986), 'Anatomy of a tomb – West Kennet revisited', *Oxford Journal of Archaeology* 5, 127–56.

6 The Sanctuary and the avenues

Cunnington, M.E. (1913), 'The re-erection of two fallen stones and the discovery of an interment with drinking cup in the Kennet Avenue', *Wiltshire Archaeological Magazine* 38, 1–8.

Cunnington, M.E. (1913), 'A buried stone on the West Kennet Avenue'. *Wiltshire Archaeological Magazine* 38, 12–14.

Cunnington, M.E. (1931), 'The 'Sanctuary' on Overton Hill, Avebury; being an account of the excavations carried out by Mr and Mrs B.H. Cunnington in 1930', *Wiltshire Archaeological Magazine* 45, 300–35.

Keiller, A.K., and Piggott, S. (1936), 'The West Kennet Avenue: excavations, 1934–5', *Antiquity* 10, 417–27.

King, B. (1879), 'Avebury: The Beckhampton Avenue', *Wiltshire Archaeological Magazine* 18, 377–83.

MacKie, E.W. (1977), *Science and Society in Prehistoric Britain*, London.

Musson, C.R. (1971), 'A study of possible building forms at Durrington Walls, Woodhenge and the Sanctuary' in Wainwright, G.J., and Longworth, I.H. (eds.), 'Durrington Walls: excavations, 1966–8', *Society of Antiquaries Research Report,* XXIX, 363–77, London.

Piggott, S. (1940), 'Timber Circles: a re-examination', *Archaeological Journal* 96, 193–222.

Thom, A., and Thom, A.S. (1976), 'Avebury: the West Kennet Avenue', *Journal of the History of Astronomy* 7, 193–7.

Vatcher, F. de M. (1969), 'Avebury: the Beckhampton Avenue', *Wiltshire Archaeological Magazine* 64, 127.

7 Silbury Hill

Atkinson, R.J.C. (1968), 'Silbury Hill', *Antiquity* 42, 299.

Atkinson, R.J.C. (1969), *Silbury Hill*, BBC supplement, BBC, London.

Atkinson, R.J.C. (1969), 'Silbury Hill', *Antiquity* 43, 00–00.

Atkinson, R.J.C. (1970), 'Silbury Hill', *Antiquity* 44, 313–4.

Brentnall, H.C. (1937–9), 'Marlborough Mount', *Wiltshire Archaeological Magazine* 48, 133-43; 140–2; 143.

Dames, M. (1976), *The Silbury Treasure: the great goddess rediscovered*, Thames and Hudson, London.

Mereweather, J. (1949), 'Examinations of Silbury Hill', *Proceedings of the Archaeological Institute, Salisbury*, 73–81.

Mereweather, J. (1851), *Diary of a Dean*, London.

Pass, A.C. (1887), 'Recent explorations at Silbury Hill', *Wiltshire Archaeological Magazine* 23, 245-254.

Petrie, Flinders, W.M. (1922), 'Diggings in Silbury, 1922', *Wiltshire Archaeological Magazine* 42, 215–18.

Smith, A.C. (1861), 'Silbury', *Wiltshire Archaeological Magazine* 7, 145–91.

Smith, A.C. (1869), 'A report of digging made in Silbury', *Wiltshire Archaeological Magazine* 11, 113–118.

8 The construction of the Great Henge

Atkinson, R.J.C. (1961), 'Prehistoric engineering', *Antiquity* 35, 292–9.

Atkinson, R.J.C. (1974), 'Ancient Astronomy: the unwritten evidence' in Hodson, F.R. (ed.), *The place of astronomy in the ancient world*, 123–124, London.

Burl, A. (1969), 'Henges: internal features and regional groups', *Archaeological Journal 126*, 1–28.

Burl, A. (1979), *Prehistoric Avebury*, Yale University Press, Yale.

Burl, A. (1983), *Prehistoric Astronomy and Ritual*, Shire Publications, Aylesbury.

Clarke, D.V., Cowie, T.G. and Foxton, A. (1985), *Symbols of power at the time of Stonehenge*, National Museum of Scotland and HMSO, London.

Passmore, A.D. (1923), 'The Langdene Stone Circle', *Wiltshire Archaeological Magazine* 42, 364–6.

Smith, I.F. (1965), *Windmill Hill and Avebury*, Clarendon Press, Oxford.

Wainwright, G.J. (1969), 'A review of henge monuments in the light of recent research', *Proceedings of the Prehistoric Society* 35, 112–33.

Wainwright, G.J. (1975), 'Religion and settlement in Wessex 3000–1700 BC' in Fowler, P.J. (ed.), *Recent work in rural archaeology*, Moonraker Press.

Wainwright, G.J., and Longworth, I.H. (1971), 'Durrington Walls: excavations 1966–68', *Reports of the research committee of the Society of Antiquaries of London* XXIX, London.

9 The Henge: later history and excavation

Aubrey, J. (1665–97), (unpublished) 'Monumenta Britannica', Bodelian Library MS Top. Gen c.24–5.

Colt Hoare, R. (1821), *Ancient Wiltshire* (II), London.

Dames, M. (1977), *The Avebury Cycle*, London.

Gray, H. St. G. (1935), 'The Avebury Excavations 1908–1922', *Archaeologia* 84, 99–162.

Hunter, J. (1829), 'The present state of Abury, Wilts', *Gentleman's Magazine* 1829, p. II, 1-7.

Hunter, M. (1975), *John Aubrey and the realm of learning*, Duckworth, London.

Keiller, A. (1939), *Guide to the Museum at Avebury, Wiltshire*. Morven Institute of Archaeological Research, Avebury.

Keiller, A., and Piggott, S. (1939), 'Avebury: summary of excavations 1937 and 1938', *Antiquity* 13, 223–33.

Passmore, A.D. (1922), 'The Avebury Ditch', *Antiquaries' Journal* 2, 109–11.

Passmore, A.D. (1935), 'The Meux excavations at Avebury', *Wiltshire Archaeological Magazine* 47, 288–9.

Piggott, S. (1964), 'Excavations at Avebury, 1960', *Wiltshire Archaeological Magazine* 59, 28–9.

Piggott, S. (1985), *William Stukeley: an eighteenth-century antiquary*, (2nd ed.), Thames and Hudson, London.

Smith, A.C. (1867), 'Excavations at Avebury', *Wiltshire Archaeological Magazine* 10, 209–16.

Smith, I.F. (1964), 'Avebury: the northern inner circle', *Wiltshire Archaeological Magazine* 59, 181.

Smith, I.F. (1965), *Windmill Hill and Avebury*, Clarendon Press, Oxford.

Stukeley, W. (1743), *Abury: a temple of the British Druids with some others described*, London.

Williamson, T., and Bellamy, L. (1983), *Ley lines in question*. World's Work Ltd., The Windmill Press, Tadworth.

Glossary

Ard Simple type of plough drawn by traction, either animal or human. Generally made of wood, with either a fire-hardened wood 'plough' tip, or a chipped stone point, set into the wooden shaft of the ard.

Avenue A processional or ceremonial way, often marked out by earth banks, standing stones or posts, usually leading from the entrance of a stone circle or henge monument.

Barrow (long) A Neolithic burial tomb of elongated shape, either constructed of earth, or a combination of earth, rubble and stone chambers. The chamber tombs often had a stone passage with smaller burial chambers opening from it, and an entrance of megalithic stones set around a semi-circular or ovoid forecourt.

Barrow (round) Usually dating from the early–mid Bronze Age, often known as a tumulus, round barrows were circular in plan, with an outer ditch, and of varied construction including disc, bowl and saucer types.

Beaker Culture Named after the beaker-shaped pots found in burials and on settlements in the final Neolithic–early Bronze Ages, from c.2400–1900 BC. The pottery was decorated with horizontal bands of finely-incised geometric decoration, and grave goods often included copper daggers and razors, flint arrowheads and scrapers, wrist guards and stone buttons. These have been interpreted as the accoutrements of an emerging warrior class at the end of the third millennium BC.

Bronze Age period following the Neolithic, from c.1800–700 BC characterized by bronze weapons and tools, round barrows, individual burials, the use of imported amber and glass and other rare materials with grave goods, and pottery ranging from food vessels to Deverill-Rimbury burial urns. The Wessex Culture forms a regional sub-group characterized by particularly rich burials such as Bush Barrow on Salisbury Plain, and the apparent emergence of a warrior-chiefly stratum of society.

Causewayed enclosures Traditionally called 'camps', these were the first major monuments built involving large numbers of people in their construction. Typical enclosures had from one to three discontinuous enclosure ditches which were interrupted by causeways between each section. Earth and rock excavated from the ditches was piled up around the inner edges of the ditches to form banks, which in some cases were supported by wooden revetments, perhaps with the intention of creating a fortified site. Enclosures appear to have had many functions, including settlements, forts, burial grounds, market places, centres of ritual activity and stock enclosures. They first appear c.3800 BC (3000 bc) and gradually declined in importance after c.2900 BC (2300 bc).

Chalk A fine-grained pure white limestone formed from small marine organisms laid down in the Cretaceous period.

Cove Setting of large standing stones at the centre of a circle or henge, often making up three sides of a rectangle, and possibly used for simple astronomical sightings and alignments.

Cursus Paired earth banks or lines of pits or stakes running parallel over an extended distance to form a rectangular earthwork, often associated with long or bank barrows and henges. They date from the mid-Neolithic period, and their purpose is unknown other than that they appear to have a ceremonial function.

Flint Silica-rich nodules formed in cretaceous chalk, exploited for prehistoric stone tools. Flint fractures into flakes suitable for chipping and grinding into tools, and forms a sharp cutting edge. The best flint was mined from seams below the ground surface at sites such as Grimes Graves (Norfolk) and Cissbury Ring (Sussex).

Greyweather A local Wiltshire term for sarsen stone, meaning sheep, since sarsens often appeared to resemble flocks of grazing sheep on the downland.

Henge monument A later Neolithic ceremonial enclosure formed by an encircling ditch and bank, with one or more causewayed entrances. Internal features included settings of stones or wooden posts in circles, alignments and circular buildings.

Neolithic period The New Stone age. It was characterized by an agricultural economy based on domesticated animals and cereals, sedentary settlement, ground stone tools and pottery. In Britain the Neolithic lasted from c.4200 BC (3400 bc) to c.2000 BC (1700 bc).

Oolitic limestone Formed predominantly from oolites, or small spherical coral bodies, dating from the Jurassic period. The Cotswolds and Calne area west of Avebury are formed from this type of rock.

Orthostats Great upright stones.

Peterborough pottery Late Neolithic style, divided into three types: the round-based, cord- and finger-impressed Mortlake; the necked bowls of Ebbsfleet with 's' shaped and carinated profiles with lattice decoration around the rims; and the flat-base, conical profile Fengate style with elaborately decorated semi-collared rims.

Post-hole Dug into the sub-soil or rock to provide a stable base for upright posts of buildings. The post-hole was packed with stones to ensure its rigidity. Evidence for the post socket can sometimes be identified when a post-hole is excavated, as a dark stain in the soil fill.

Radio-carbon dating or C14 A method of dating any once-living matter. The carbon dioxide in the air contains a small amount of C14 radio isotope, produced by bombardments of nitrogen with cosmic rays. This is incorporated in living organisms during their lifetime, but once it dies, the amount of C14 present begins to decrease due to beta decay into nitrogen 14. The amount of radio-carbon present may be measured in a counter to give an estimate of the object's age. The half-life of C14 is 5730 years, making the method suitable for dating objects up to about 10,000 years old. The estimated date of the object is then calibrated against a comparative calendar derived from tree ring dates. Uncalibrated dates are expressed as 'bc' whereas calendar dates are express- as BC.

Sarsen A hard sandstone rock derived from a silicaceous sand formed above the cretaceous chalk about 30–20 million years ago. Following geological movement, chemical metamorphosis and weathering, the sandstone was broken into blocks and deposited over the chalk downland and valleys. The very hard stone provided a local supply of suitable material for Neolithic megaliths, as standing stones and in chambered tombs, and also as querns and grindstones for stone tools. Sarsens were used at Avebury, Stonehenge and in several other Neolithic monuments.

Silt Fine-grained deposit of clay, fine sand and soil particles that tend to wash down slopes into pockets and valleys, forming a fertile and easily-worked soil for agriculture.

Windmill Hill culture Earlier-middle Neolithic culture characterized by a distinctive pottery style. Pottery includes several sub-groups from the southern Britain, including Hembury ware, Abingdon and Mildenhall. Early Windmill Hill ware was plain with round-based 'baggy' profiles and rolled-over rims. Later Windmill Hill ware included incised and punched decoration around and below the rim, and had handles and lugs. Hembury ware had distinctive tubular handles and Abingdon ware had distinctive thickened and rolled-over rims with slightly carinated profiles which had incised or stamped impressions as decorations. The easterly Mildenhall style had wide-mouthed carinated bowls, with thickened rims and ornament on the shoulder of the vessel.

Index